D1231998

NUCLEAR WASTE

NUCLEAR WASTE

THE 10,000-YEAR CHALLENGE

BY EDWARD F. DOLAN AND
MARGARET M. SCARIANO

Franklin Watts/1990
New York/London/Toronto/Sydney

363.72 14256
Dol
3-25-91

Diagrams by Vantage Art

Photographs courtesy of: UPI/Bettmann Newsphotos: pp. 22, 26, 68, 77, 118, 135; AP/Wide World Photos: pp. 34 top, 41, 42, 45, 52, 123; Department of Energy: pp. 34 bottom, 97, 107; Monkmeyer Press Photo: p. 88 (Mimi Forsyth); Radioactive Waste Campaign: p. 126.

Library of Congress Cataloging-in-Publication Data

Dolan, Edward F., 1924–
  Nuclear Waste : the 10,000-year challenge / by Edward F. Dolan and Margaret M. Scariano.
    p. cm.
  Includes bibliographical references.
  Summary: Examines the causes of nuclear waste, the threats it poses to human health and the environment, and efforts to regulate its disposal.
  ISBN 0-531-10943-7
  1. Radioactive wastes—Juvenile literature. 2. Radioactive pollution—Environmental aspects—Juvenile literature. [1. Radioactive wastes. 2. Radioactive pollution. 3. Pollution.] I. Scariano, Margaret. II. Title.
  TD898.D64 1990
  363.72'89—dc20   90-34586 CIP AC

For Frank and Rose

ACKNOWLEDGMENTS

We are indebted to many people for their help in the preparation of this book. In particular, for providing us with much research material and patiently answering specific questions, a special word of appreciation must go to: Dilip Bhadra, physicist and staff scientist, General Atomic Company, San Diego, California; the public information staff of the Office of Civilian Radioactive Waste Management, U.S. Department of Energy, Washington, D.C.; the Battelle organization, Pacific Northwest Laboratories, Richland, Washington; Lt. Col. (USMC, Ret.) Austin B. Middleton of Concept RKK, Ltd., Bellevue, Washington; the office of U.S. Representative Barbara Boxer, 5th Congressional District, California. Our special thanks also go to Professor Joe O. Ledbetter of the College of Engineering at the University of Texas at Austin for reviewing our manuscript and making many fine and helpful editorial comments.

CONTENTS

NUCLEAR WASTE

INTRODUCTION

THE 10,000-YEAR CHALLENGE

The age of nuclear energy, now almost a half century old, has given the world a great source of energy for both good and evil. On the one hand, it has helped to provide the electric power that does so much to make our lives more productive and enjoyable. On the other hand, it has terrorized us with the awful weapons it has created.

Ranking high among its most frightening aspects are the waste materials that result from the production of nuclear energy. Nuclear wastes loom as a danger to life and the environment because they are radioactive, emitting a radiation that can be deadly. Adding to their dangers is the fact that many require up to an astonishing 10,000 years before their radiation dwindles to the point where they are no longer able to harm.

Today more than twenty-five nations around the world, the United States among them, use nuclear energy as a power source. They have all accumulated many tons of waste materials over the years. The wastes cannot be burned out of existence or simply thrown aside and forgotten. To burn or carelessly discard the wastes would cause them to release their radiation and poison the world's air, land, water, and myriad life-forms—our own included.

And so, today's nuclear nations, and those of the future, face a tremendous challenge. They must find ways to store the wastes so that they are safely locked away from life and the environment for as long as their power to destroy lasts—as long as 10,000 years for the most dangerous of those wastes. In this book, we are going to look at what the nuclear nations, especially the United States, are doing to meet this long-term challenge.

Just as the danger of nuclear wastes threatens all of us, so should the challenge of safely storing nuclear wastes concern us all—not just our government. If we fail to meet the challenge, if we ignore the dangers that threaten the health and well-being of our world, then we or our descendants may one day face the consequences of that failure.

1

THE NUCLEAR AGE

The day was Monday, August 6, 1945. At eight o'clock in the morning, the United States Air Force bomber *Enola Gay* approached the Japanese city of Hiroshima.[1] Minutes later, the aircraft roared in above the heart of the city. A thick-bodied, 10-foot-long projectile—packed with an explosive power equal to some 20,000 tons of TNT and soon to be known worldwide as an atomic bomb—dropped from the ship's underbelly. Hiroshima was lost from view in a blinding flash that, upon fading, revealed a mushroom-shaped cloud churning thousands of feet into the air. Left below was a devastated, burning city, with thousands of its people incinerated.

Three days later, another U.S. bomber, *Bock's Car,* swept in over the city of Nagasaki, not far from Hiroshima. There was another blinding flash, another boiling cloud, and thousands of lives were lost—all caused by a single atomic bomb.

As a result of those two explosions and the radioactive mushroom clouds that followed them, some

210,000 Japanese people died. Uncounted others were left maimed and sick for life. On August 15, 1945, Japan surrendered, and World War II came to a close with this abrupt end of the war's Pacific phase. (The war in Europe had ended with the surrender of Japan's ally Germany a few months earlier.) As word of what had happened to Hiroshima and Nagasaki spread, people of all nations were jolted by the realization that they had been thrust suddenly into a new and frightening era. The age of nuclear energy or, as it was then called, the atomic age, had begun.

THE NUCLEAR AGE

Ever since the birth of the nuclear age, people everywhere have been frightened by the potentially harmful nature of nuclear energy. But that energy has also impressed us with its potential for good. On the one hand, we have watched with dread as the United States, the Soviet Union, and other nations have used nuclear energy to develop increasingly potent weapons (like the hydrogen bomb), all with a destructive power infinitely greater than that inflicted on Hiroshima and Nagasaki. On the other hand, we have seen nuclear energy harnessed for peaceful and beneficial commercial purposes. Its greatest commercial use has been to provide nations around the world with a new source of electric power.

But even the development of nuclear energy for peaceful civilian use has been a source of fear because it involves the production of radioactive materials. These materials give off a radiation that, when strong enough, can prove deadly to humans, animals, and the environment.

Equaling this fear is another—the fear that has prompted the writing of this book. As do other industrial processes, the manufacture of nuclear energy leaves behind waste products. Nuclear wastes, which take the form of gases, liquids, and solid matter, are hazardous because they, too, emit radiation that can be deadly. They pose other dangers as well. There is great concern today that, as the result of the growing use of nuclear power over the years, the wastes have accumulated to the point where they have the potential to do worldwide harm to our health and our environment.

However, before we can truly understand the potential dangers of nuclear wastes and see what must be done to safeguard ourselves from them, we need to have a basic knowledge of nuclear energy and its benefits and hazards.

NUCLEAR ENERGY: HARNESSING ITS POWER

The term *nuclear energy* comes from the word *nucleus.*[2] The nucleus is a speck of matter at the center of an atom. It is composed mainly of electrically charged particles called *protons* and nonelectrical particles called *neutrons.* Nuclear energy is generated when the nuclei (the plural of "nucleus") in the atoms of certain substances are made to change their composition. The nuclei are altered by having their atomic number, mass number, or radioactivity changed. For definitions of these terms, see the glossary at the end of the book.

Nuclear energy can be released from the nuclei in two ways. As diagrammed in Figure 1, the first method is called *fission,* which means "splitting." Also known as fissioning, it is the process used to produce electric power. It employs substances containing atoms

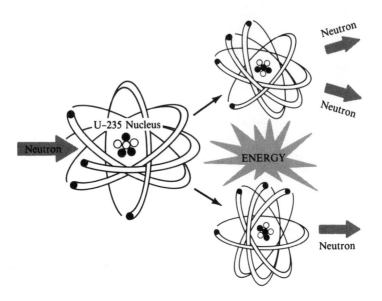

Figure 1. How Fission Works
It takes about a millionth of a second for a neutron to strike the
nucleus of a uranium–235 atom. This causes the atom to break apart
and release energy and more neutrons. If these neutrons hit other
U–235 atoms, within seconds, what results is a nuclear chain reaction,
with millions of atoms fissioning and releasing a lot of heat.

of a heavy weight. The fissioning substance used
worldwide today is U-235, a form of the metal uranium, whose ore is mined in such locales as Africa,
Canada, and the United States. U-235's nuclei split
open when struck by an outside neutron. This breaking
releases two or three neutrons, which then split open
still other nuclei so that they, too, are altered and the
energy released. This continuous splitting is called a
chain reaction.

The second method is *fusion.* Here, the energy is
created by fusing (joining) the nuclei of certain atoms
rather than splitting them. Both U-235 and the element plutonium-239 are used in the process. Scientists
have not yet been able to harness fusion for the pro-

duction of electricity. At present, it is used only in the manufacture of nuclear weapons by the United States government and various other countries.

NUCLEAR ENERGY:
ITS BENEFITS

Fission releases a vast amount of heat from the tiny nuclei. The heat is triggered in nuclear reactors, which are the tanklike installations in which fissioning takes place. In turn, this nuclear energy heats the water circulating in the reactors and thus creates the steam that drives the turbines in electric generators. In turn, the generators provide electricity to homes and buildings and the power to drive industrial machinery. When generated by smaller reactors, the nuclear energy powers ships and submarines.

In the years since World War II, more than twenty-five nations, operating more than 300 nuclear plants, have put this fission-produced heat to use to generate electric power.[3] The countries are located on all continents. They include France, Great Britain, and West Germany in Europe; Bahrain and Israel in the Middle East; Australia, China, Japan, and New Zealand in the Asia-Pacific area; Algeria and Egypt in Africa; Argentina, Canada, Mexico, and the United States in the western hemisphere; and the Soviet Union, which lies in both Europe and Asia.

A Valuable Power Source
For three reasons, nuclear energy is of great value in the production of power.[4]

1. It is a less expensive energy source than the fossil fuels—coal, oil, and gas—that have long provided the world with power. Electricity produced from uranium

is more than six times cheaper than electricity produced from oil or coal.

2. Nuclear energy is a far cleaner source than the fossil fuels. Though its radiation is dangerous if not properly contained, nuclear energy does not dirty the air with pollutants. The burning of fossil fuels in factories and automobile engines is currently adding more than 5.5 billion tons of polluting carbon dioxide to the world's atmosphere each year.

3. Nuclear energy works far more efficiently than the fossil fuels because of its ability to generate massive power from small amounts of a substance. One gram of uranium creates as much power as the burning of 3 tons of coal. But the earth's supply of uranium, like its supply of fossil fuels, is limited. However, because so little uranium is required to generate so much power, the supply promises to last a long time, in contrast to the earth's rapidly dwindling supply of fossil fuels.

The world's first nuclear reactor was built for experimental purposes at the University of Chicago in 1942. In 1957 the United States built its first nuclear reactor for electric power. Since then, the number of the nation's reactors has grown to 114 (as of late 1989). A map indicating the rough locations of the nation's nuclear reactors as of August 1988 is provided in Figure 2. Located in more than thirty states, they provide an estimated 18 to 20 percent of all the electricity produced in the United States. Nuclear energy produces some 15 percent of the world's electric power.

A Valuable Medical Tool
Nuclear energy has proven to be so valuable in the medical field that it has given rise to a distinct branch of medicine known as nuclear medicine. Nuclear en-

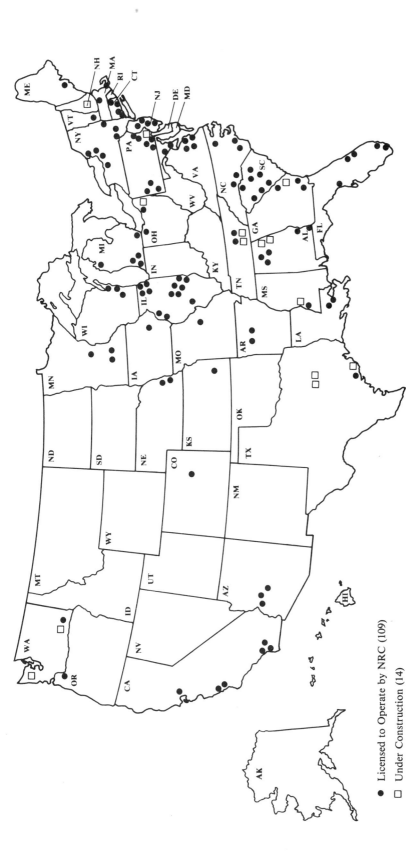

Source: *Managing The Nation's Nuclear Waste* August 1988
U.S. Department of Energy

- Licensed to Operate by NRC (109)
- Under Construction (14)
★ Planned (0)

Symbols do not reflect precise locations due to space limitations

Figure 2. Nuclear Reactors in the United States

ergy is widely used in the treatment of various physical disabilities and illnesses, including some types of cancer.

One of its most recent medical applications has been in the improvement of the pacemaker, an instrument that is surgically implanted in the chest of many heart patients to steady and control the heartbeat. America's first nuclear-powered pacemaker was implanted in a patient in 1988. Driven by a minuscule amount of plutonium, it is expected to operate for twenty to forty years, whereas ordinary pacemakers powered by small electric batteries have a life expectancy of only five to eight years. The long service rendered by the nuclear-powered pacemaker eliminates the need for frequent surgical replacement.

NUCLEAR ENERGY: ITS TERRORS

Despite its benefits, nuclear energy for civilian use continues to be deeply feared because of the radiation given off by its radioactive elements.[5] Many people think that all radiation is dangerous, but this is not true.

Radiation has always existed on our planet. Every day we are all exposed to radiation from various natural sources and absorb it without harm. U.S. citizens yearly receive radiation averaging out at 160.81 millirem.* About 67.6 percent of this amount is received from the sun and earth. About 30.7 percent comes from such radiation-emitting devices as medical and

---

* A millirem is one-thousandth of a rem. The rem is a basic measurement of the effects of a dose of radiation on human tissue. In scientific circles, a new term is beginning to replace the rem as a basic measure of radiation dosage—the Sievert (Sv). One Sievert equals approximately 100 rem.

dental X-ray machines. What is called miscellaneous radiation adds up to 1.7 percent of the total.

Some people, because they work or live a little closer to the sun than others, are exposed to amounts of radiation above the national average. Airline personnel who fly about sixty hours a month usually receive some 160 millirem more radiation than the average citizen. Workers in the nuclear power industry absorb about 400 millirem above the average.

All this radiation is safely absorbed because it is received in minuscule amounts over extended periods of time. But things change when too much radiation is absorbed in a short time, either from an exploding nuclear bomb or in a mishap at a reactor plant. Once the radioactive elements are in the atmosphere, their radiation can seriously damage the cells that make up all living things.

Radiation can burn; one victim of the Hiroshima bombing was so scorched that his fingers were fused together. It can bring on skin and internal cancers and can trigger other problems in various organs. It can cause birth defects in the children of its victims. And it can induce what is called radiation sickness—an often fatal illness that attacks the bone marrow, gastrointestinal tract, and central nervous system and causes weakness, diarrhea, fever, chills, boils, vomiting, the loss of hair, and a dramatic decrease in the white corpuscles in the blood. White corpuscles are blood cells that help us fight off disease and illness.

Sudden large doses of radiation can kill. A dose of 10,000 rem attacks the central nervous system and may cause swift death. A dose of 300 to 500 rem is said to kill about 50 percent of the time. Doses from 100 to 300 rem are likely to cause radiation injury. The diagram in Figure 3 shows the harmful effects of radiation sickness in the human body.

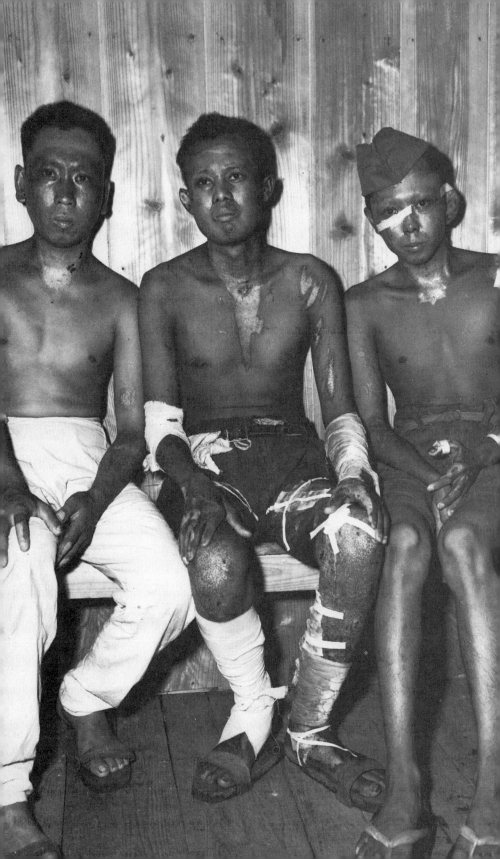

There are also terrible dangers present when the unleashed radiation seeps into the ground, contaminating the earth itself, its rock formations, its plant life, and its surface and underground water supply. The afflicted area is made unfit for human and animal habitation.

These awful facts have caused us to worry about every aspect of the manufacture of nuclear energy for either civilian or military use: Are our reactors well built, or do they have flaws in their design and construction that will one day allow too much deadly radiation to escape? What are the chances of accidents taking place at the reactor sites?

A number of reactor mishaps in recent years have shown us that we have good reason to worry.

Reactor Mishaps: The Chernobyl Tragedy
The worst peacetime nuclear mishap occurred on April 24, 1986, at the Chernobyl nuclear plant in the Soviet Union's Ukraine region.[6] An explosion and fire split open one of the reactors and caused a core meltdown. The core is the heart of a nuclear reactor, the area that contains the atoms being fissioned and the highly radioactive fission products. Because of the great heat generated by the fissioning, the core must be kept cool at all times by circulating water or gas around it. When deprived of the needed coolant, the

These young men display the burns they received when an atomic bomb exploded over the city of Nagasaki. Note how their clothing protected parts of their bodies.

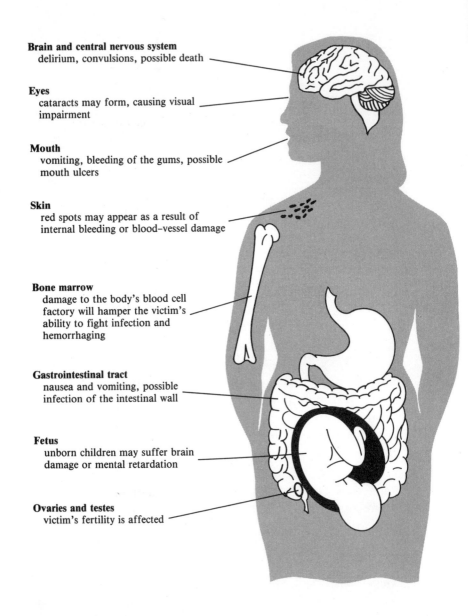

Brain and central nervous system
delirium, convulsions, possible death

Eyes
cataracts may form, causing visual impairment

Mouth
vomiting, bleeding of the gums, possible mouth ulcers

Skin
red spots may appear as a result of internal bleeding or blood–vessel damage

Bone marrow
damage to the body's blood cell factory will hamper the victim's ability to fight infection and hemorrhaging

Gastrointestinal tract
nausea and vomiting, possible infection of the intestinal wall

Fetus
unborn children may suffer brain damage or mental retardation

Ovaries and testes
victim's fertility is affected

Figure 3. Effects of Acute Radiation Sickness
What can happen when a person is exposed to high doses of ionizing radiation?

core quickly overheats—or "melts down"—with the result that too much radiation is allowed to escape.

The meltdown that occurred in Chernobyl hurled 7 tons of radioactive debris into the atmosphere. High winds carried the hazardous material as far away as Sweden and Great Britain to the west, and Italy and Turkey to the south. The Soviet government reported that the blast killed two people and hospitalized 197 with injuries. Thousands of others in the USSR and elsewhere were exposed to increased levels of radiation. An area of 2,500 square kilometers around the plant was rendered uninhabitable by the radioactivity.

The economic effects of the Chernobyl explosion are still being felt in widely separated areas. In Turkey, homegrown tea remains unsafe to drink. Food grown in central Sweden and northern Italy is unfit to eat. Vast numbers of sheep in Scotland and reindeer in Scandinavia's Lappland are unmarketable because they have been contaminated with radiation.

Even worse is the toll on human life. Within three months of the explosion, twenty-eight people in the damaged region were reported dead of radiation poisoning; 300 were treated for serious radiation exposure. A study made in 1988 estimated that, as a result of the accident, the next fifty years will bring 6,500 additional cancer deaths to the Soviet people living outside the Chernobyl area. Beyond the USSR's borders, an additional 10,400 deaths from cancer are predicted for Europe during that same period. Five hundred are predicted for Asia, and fewer than 100 for Canada and the United States. Still, these projected figures constitute only a minute fraction of the total cancer deaths that can be expected in the next half century—35 million for the Soviet Union, 342 million

for Asia, and 49 million for Canada and the United States combined.

Another recent study of the Chernobyl disaster has revealed that the occurrence of lip, mouth, and other cancers has doubled among the residents of a nearby farm area. One Soviet newspaper has reported that half the children in the Narodichsky region of the Ukraine now suffer from an unusually high number of thyroid problems. Such conditions can be caused by heavy radiation exposure. Another newspaper has said that calves in the Chernobyl area are being born without heads and limbs and that the number of birth defects in animals has been rising yearly since that terrible April day in 1986.

Reactor Mishaps in the United States
The United States has also suffered several accidents at nuclear plants, though none as serious as the Chernobyl mishap.[7] In March 1979, at the Three Mile Island nuclear plant in Middletown, Pennsylvania, a valve part worth just fifteen cents failed to operate in one of the reactors. Before the malfunction was discovered, it caused several hundred thousand gallons of vital cooling water around the core to escape, with the result that the core sustained a partial meltdown. Some radiation escaped into the air, but fortunately no one

An engineer from the U.S. Department of Energy tests water samples along the Susquehanna River for radioactivity. In the background lies the Three Mile Island nuclear plant, where a radioactive leakage occurred in 1979.

died or was injured in the mishap. However, since the accident, people living near the installation have feared that they may be suffering from illnesses that have yet to surface.

Other accidents that have occurred in the United States include the following:

- A steam explosion in 1961 killed three workers at a military experimental reactor in Idaho. There was heavy radiation inside the plant, but the danger was brought under control.

- In 1979, a top-secret nuclear plant in Tennessee accidentally released a highly potent form of uranium. About 1,000 people were struck with five times the radiation they would ordinarily receive in a year.

- A cylinder of uranium was improperly heated at an Oklahoma nuclear plant in 1986, and small amounts of radiation escaped into the atmosphere. One worker died, and 100 others were hospitalized.

All of those accidents occurred at U.S. government installations. Despite such accidents, the U.S. Department of Energy (DOE),* which oversees the government's work with nuclear energy, claims that the United States can boast an excellent safety record during the years since the first American reactor was built. Plant accidents have caused only four deaths, and the DOE recently reported that not one member of the

* The agency in charge of commercial uses of nuclear energy in the United States is the Nuclear Regulatory Commission.

American public has been killed or injured by radiation from a reactor failure or accident.

But this safety record is of little comfort to many Americans. They fear that a Chernobyl-like disaster can strike any of the country's commercial and military reactors at any moment. They fear that the escape of radiation from plants such as that at Three Mile Island—and others that will be discussed later in this book—will damage the surrounding environment and threaten the health and lives of humans and animals.

At present, there are 114 commercial and 17 government nuclear plants operating in the United States, and 16 more commercial installations are being planned. But widespread public fear has led to the abandonment of plans for more than fifty new commercial plants. It is a fear shared by countless people in other countries, where a number of nuclear facilities have been closed and the planning for new additions canceled.

Is this concern justified? Is nuclear energy indeed too volatile to be completely tamed? Or, as the future brings about the development of new technologies and safeguards, will nuclear power eventually become not a menace but a power source as reliable as electricity is today? Only time will tell.

NUCLEAR WASTE: CONCERNS AND QUESTIONS

Armed now with a background in nuclear energy, we can return to the subject of this book, nuclear waste. We fear the gaseous, liquid, and solid nuclear waste materials, of course, because of their radiation. But much of our fear is the result of our ignorance. The fact is that most of us know little or nothing about the wastes and the hazards they do—or do not—threaten for us. Until recently, almost the only people who knew about nuclear waste were those who worked in or lived near civilian or military nuclear plants. But now, as the number of waste products grows yearly with the continuing use of nuclear energy, the subject of nuclear waste is becoming more familiar and worrisome to many more of us. We have become deeply concerned for a number of reasons.

We wonder if the radiation from nuclear waste has the same power to kill and sicken as the radiation loosed in a nuclear explosion or reactor accident. We wonder if the waste materials themselves can explode and tear a reactor plant apart. And we wonder about the danger of their radiation entering the atmosphere, the ground, or our water supply—not from explosion or accident, but via seepage from the piles of waste products that have been accumulating through the years at plant sites and other locations.

Finally, there is particular concern over that word *accumulating.* Nuclear wastes have been accumulating over the years because we cannot dispose of them as we do many other industrial wastes. We cannot, for example, burn them or wash them away in a river. Burning would poison the air with their deadly radiation and washing them away would just as lethally pollute our drinking water.

Disposal is possible only through what is called *shielding.* This means the storing away of the wastes so that they are securely beyond our reach. They must be placed in storage facilities that will provide maximum protection against the escape of their radioactivity for many years—in some cases, thousands of years.

The concerns of people around the world about

nuclear waste and the need for its safe storage have taken the form of questions like these:

- Exactly how dangerous are the various waste products? Are they all equally dangerous? Which of them should we fear most?

- Have the wastes been stored wisely or carelessly in the past? Are they being properly stored at present?

- If stored carelessly, have they already harmed us?

- What is being done to insure that they will be safely stored throughout the future?

We are now going to look at these and other concerns and questions. Let's begin with a look at the waste itself so that we can become well acquainted with the enemy.

2

IT'S CALLED
RADWASTE

Nuclear waste consists of by-products—"extra" materials that are generated and left over during the various processes that go into the making of nuclear energy.[1] Some waste materials are produced in the mining of nuclear ores. Some are generated in reactors during the fissioning process. Others take shape during the development and manufacture of nuclear weapons and in the research aimed at improving nuclear equipment and production techniques. And still others crop up during the preparation of nuclear medicines.

Regardless of where these assorted wastes come from, they all present the same problem: contamination by radioactivity.

In what ways have they been contaminated?[2] Some, such as the fuel rods used in the fissioning process, have been saturated with high-powered radioactivity. These rods are stainless steel or zirconium cylinders in which uranium pellets are placed for fissioning. The rods measure 3 to 14 feet long and about a half inch in diameter. They are bundled together in units of

30 to 300 rods and inserted into the reactor core. Each bundle is known as a fuel assembly.

Various numbers of fuel assemblies are placed in reactors, depending on the size of the reactor. In time, the assemblies become so shot through with radioactivity that they can no longer perform efficiently and must be replaced (usually every two to three years). The replaced assemblies, their rods, and their uranium contents are listed as wastes and are called, in turn, spent fuel assemblies, spent fuel rods, and spent fuels. The assemblies and rods are highly dangerous wastes because they are saturated with the various radionuclides that are created during fissioning.

What are radionuclides? When the U-235 nuclei split open during fissioning, their composition is changed, and they become a string of new elements. Among these new elements are plutonium-239 (which is used in the manufacture of nuclear weapons), strontium-90, and cesium-137. Since the new elements are created in a reactor rather than in nature, they are said to be man-made. They are composed of nuclides that are called radionuclides because they are radioactive. (A nuclide is a type of atom that is characterized by the makeup of its nucleus—namely by the number of protons and neutrons and the energy content in the nucleus.)

Other materials employed in nuclear production are turned into waste products when they become contaminated by radionuclides and are rendered too dangerous for further use by humans. Examples of these kinds of waste are many. They range from the protective clothing worn by nuclear workers—gloves, shoes, masks, and the like—to hand tools of all sorts and even wiping rags and such personal possessions as handkerchiefs.

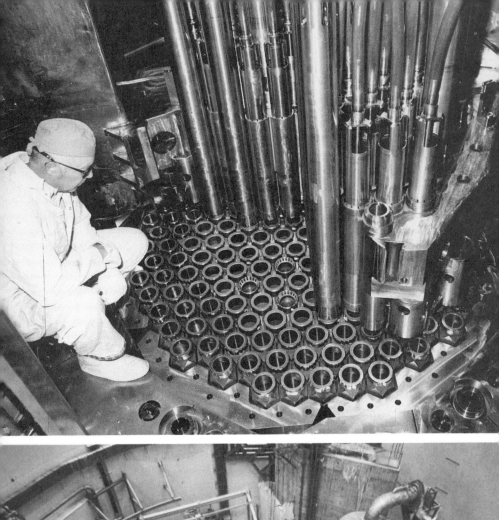

The waste materials resulting from all phases of nuclear production can be so numerous that they seem beyond count. They can be gases, liquids, or solid objects. Because of their great number, they were long ago lumped together under a single term: radwaste.

TYPES OF RADWASTE

The U.S. Department of Energy (DOE) divides the various items of radwaste into four types.[3] Each type is established on the basis of where its waste materials originated, the intensity of its radiation, the length of time its radioactivity lasts, and its potential dangers to life and the environment. None of these types will ever explode on their own; they are not capable of detonating themselves. Should a reactor or a nuclear weapon containing radwastes explode while the wastes are in it, the wastes will become dangerous upon being spewed into the atmosphere. Their principal danger lurks in the amount of radiation they emit.

The four types of radwaste are: high-level waste, low-level waste, transuranic waste, and mill tailings. For the purposes of this book, the most important are the high-level and low-level wastes. The most dangerous of all is high-level waste.

(Top) An engineer studies the fuel rods of a new reactor's fuel core during its installation. (Bottom) An overhead view of a working reactor core (center), flanked by four steam generators.

High-Level Waste

High-level waste (HLW) is generated during the production of nuclear energy for both civilian and military purposes. Much of it comes from the spent fuels—the U-235 and the radionuclides that have saturated the fuel rods and assemblies during fissioning.

HLW is also generated in the reprocessing of spent fuels. Reprocessing is the method by which U-235 and plutonium-239 are removed chemically from a fuel assembly so that they can be reused. Reprocessing results in a liquid waste. This waste can be converted into a solid by evaporating its water content; the solid remains behind as residue. Another type of liquid waste is the water coolant that keeps a reactor from overheating.

High-level waste generates a great heat and emits a dangerous radiation. It requires remote handling, which means that there must be no human contact with it, and it must be stored in a dense material if we are to be safely shielded from its radiation. The materials that do the best job of shielding are lead, concrete, steel, or water.

The radiation that results from the production of nuclear energy is principally of three invisible types—alpha, beta, and gamma. These radiations are born when nuclear materials explode, break down, or disintegrate during fissioning or fusion. The three are also found in nature—in rocks, soils, and minerals—and we are able to absorb their radiation safely. These radiations also serve useful purposes. Gamma radiations, for instance, play a part in medical X rays and are found in the luminous dials of wristwatches. The radiations become dangerous when, as in nuclear production, they are generated in heavy concentrations. High-level waste, laced as it is with U-235 and various radionuclides, emits the three radiations in great amounts, with the most potentially dangerous radiation coming from the gammas. Gammas are especially hazardous because, since they consist of high-energy electromagnetic waves, they are highly penetrating and can pass easily through the human body. It is because of their penetrating abilities that dense materials must be used to shield us from high-level wastes.

Alpha radiations, which consist of positively-charged particles, are actually far more injurious to the body than the gammas and betas, but fortunately their penetration is weak and can be stopped by a sheet of paper or the outer layer of one's skin. Beta radiations are composed of particles similar to electrons and are slightly more penetrating than the alphas. They are able to pass through human skin or about an inch of water. A thin sheet of aluminum, however, can halt their penetration.

Once formed, the high-level wastes begin to decay (as do the other types of nuclear waste). This means that they lose their radioactivity over a period of time. Eventually they change into more harmless substances, until at last the radioactivity drops to a level where it no longer poses a threat to life and the environment.

The various radioactive elements, however, decay at different rates of speed. Some drop to safe levels in seconds, minutes, days, weeks, or months. Spent fuels and other high-level wastes lose about 50 percent of their radioactivity after about three months in storage, and approximately 80 percent after one year. But the radiation from certain radionuclides persists at dangerous levels for lengths of time that can stagger the imagination—hundreds to thousands of years. It can take about 10,000 years for the remaining radioactivity in some HLW to drop to a safe level—that is, the level at which the radioactivity in the waste is comparable to that of the uranium ore that was mined for fissioning.*

Low-Level Waste
Low-level waste (LLW) is generated wherever radioactive materials are used. It is produced in such facilities as reactor plants; industrial plants; hospitals; and government, university, and commercial laboratories devoted to nuclear research and development. The waste material is as varied as the installations that produce it. To the list of materials mentioned earlier (everything from protective clothing to small hand tools and wiping rags) must be added such items as large scale equipment, laboratory test tubes, and the carcasses of animals used in nuclear research.

As its name suggests, low-level waste is much less dangerous than high-level waste. It contains radioactive elements with low hazard levels and fast decay rates. Their radiation drops to safe levels in anything from a few seconds to a few months. However, radiation from some low-level wastes is high enough to require that they be encased in a dense material and shielded from workers for a time. LLW can usually be safely stored by shallow burial. The burial must be made with care in locations that are controlled so that they will not be used indiscriminately by nuclear workers or the public.

Overall, the danger of radiation from LLW is not great. The waste is principally dangerous when, for

---

* Scientists use the term *half-life* to measure the time needed for a radioactive substance to decay to the point of safety. A half-life is defined as the amount of time that half the atoms in a particular element take to lose their radioactivity.

some reason, a person touches or swallows it or inhales its fumes.

Transuranic Waste

Transuranic waste (TRU) results mainly from the reprocessing of spent nuclear fuels and from the use of plutonium-239 in the making of nuclear weapons. They are so-named because they have been contaminated by transuranics, which include certain nuclides of plutonium and various forms of uranium.

Transuranic wastes are characterized by a moderately penetrating radiation and a fairly lengthy decay time. When their transuranic content is great enough, it can take more than twenty years for their radiation to reach a safe level. This lengthy decay time requires that the wastes be as securely stored as the high-level wastes. Because of their moderate penetration abilities, however, TRUs need little or no shielding or remote handling.

Not much transuranic waste is to be found in the United States because there has been no reprocessing of the spent fuels from American civilian reactors since 1977. That year the federal government banned civilian reprocessing, mainly because of the fear that the plutonium being extracted might be stolen by a terrorist group or a foreign power and then used to fashion nuclear weapons. The ban was lifted in 1981, but the civilian nuclear plants did not resume reprocessing because of the great expense involved. Spent fuels, however, are being reprocessed in defense reactors because both uranium and plutonium are used in nuclear weaponry.

Mill Tailings

Uranium mill tailings consist of earthen residues left over from the mining of uranium ore and the extraction of uranium from the ore. Made up of soil and fine sand, they contain low-level concentrations of such naturally occurring radioactive substances as radium-226 and thorium-230. The mill tailings emit the radioactive gas radon-222 (which is created by the decay of their radium content) and some gamma rays. As they decay, the wastes also give off alpha and beta radiation.

In the western hemisphere, uranium is mined in Canada and the United States. There are more than 200 million tons of radioactive mill-tailings in the United States, all of it stored in sparsely populated areas of such western states as Arizona, New Mexico, Utah, and Wyoming. The DOE, in a recent publication, claims that all piles of mill tailings have been buried to shield the radon emissions. In 1989, however, *National Geographic* magazine reported that the amount of stored mill tailings in the United States has prompted a widespread public call for a campaign to clear them away.

HOW MUCH RADWASTE IS THERE?

As the most important waste categories for the purposes of this book are the high-level and low-level types, let's look now at how much waste of each type has been accumulated in the United States over the years.[4]

Steel drums containing low-level nuclear waste are dumped into a 30-foot-deep trench at a northwest Illinois disposal facility.

HLW Accumulation

Compared to the power that its contents have helped to create, high-level waste is produced in small quantities. Anywhere from 1 to 100 cubic meters (a cubic meter is roughly equivalent to a cubic yard) of HLW is created annually by a reactor turning out 1,000 million watts of power. Over the years, the nation's civilian and defense nuclear operations have collected more than 310,000 cubic meters of high-level waste, with most (over 306,000 cubic meters) coming from government installations. The waste is made up of spent fuel assemblies, water from the government reprocessing of spent fuels for defense purposes, and other materials.

At present, the weight of spent fuel assemblies from U.S. commercial reactors adds up to more than 15,000 metric tons. By the year 2000, the accumulation is expected to stand at more than double its present weight, or a total of 40,000 or more metric tons. Added to the civilian total can be another 8,000 to 10,000 metric tons of HLW generated at defense nuclear plants. (Much of the government high-level waste is presently in liquid form. The tonnage is computed on the weight of the waste when solidified.)

The present spent-fuel tonnage from civilian reactors is sufficient to cover a football field to a depth of three feet.

LLW Accumulation

Because they are found wherever nuclear materials are used, and because they consist of so many different

This Los Alamos facility serves as a temporary storage site for containers that hold transuranic waste.

items, LLWs are generated in far greater quantities than HLWs—roughly 1,000 to 10,000 cubic meters per year from a reactor turning out 1,000 million watts of power.

At present, well over 3 million cubic meters of low-level wastes have been accumulated by both civilian and defense nuclear installations. Of that total, the government facilities are responsible for upwards of 2 million cubic meters. By the year 2000, the total civilian and defense accumulation is expected to be in the neighborhood of 7 million cubic meters, with the total divided about equally between the civilian and government operations.

Two points are now beginning to be clear. They are:

- High level waste, with its penetrating and long-lived radiation (a radiation that can take up to 10,000 years to decay to a safe level) must be *more than* securely and safely stored. It must be *permanently* stored away from contact with life and the environment.

- Although low-level waste is characterized by low levels and generally short lifespans of radi-

Navajo residents are asked to avoid using a nearby river for drinking or watering their animals during a cleanup effort following a uranium tailings spill in New Mexico.

WARNING
ALL USE OF WATER FROM
THIS RIVER IS DISCOURAGED
BY THE N.M.E.I.D.
AVISO
"N.M.E.I.D.
NO RECOMIENDA EL USO
DE AGUA DE ESTE RIO."
BÁ HÁ DZID
N.M.E.I.D. WOLYE
DÉGO ADANI DI TÓ CHOO II
DOLEEŁIIGE DO BE HASAADA

ation, some of it can be strong enough to be a hazard for extended periods of time. Consequently, much of it must be stored as *permanently* as the HLWs.

The need for safe and permanent storage has haunted the nuclear waste story throughout its history. It is a need that went long ignored in a history that began with what can now be called "the blind years."

3

THE BLIND YEARS

Considering what we now know of the hazards of nuclear wastes, it seems hard to believe that these wastes were once handled and stored carelessly in the United States. But such was the case at the dawn of the nuclear era. In fairness, however, we cannot call the carelessness of that time a matter of stupid negligence. Rather, it was the result of an ignorance on the part of many of our nuclear experts.

WHY THE IGNORANCE?

Our ignorance was understandable for a number of reasons.[1] First, in the beginning, nuclear wastes were as new as nuclear energy itself, so there was little understanding of their dangers. No one fully realized just how hazardous nuclear wastes really were and how great their hazards would become as the use of the energy burgeoned in the coming years. Second, the amounts of waste being generated at the start were small. Most scientists were confident that as the amounts of waste accumulated over coming years, methods for their efficient disposal would be developed. In the meantime, the nuclear installations were to handle their wastes as they saw fit.

Third, during the opening years of the era, the nation concentrated on the development of nuclear power for military and then civilian purposes. With all the attention focused on development, there was little time left over to think of the wastes. They went ignored.

In fact, all the initial attention was riveted on nuclear weaponry, at first for use in World War II and then for the nation's defense and security. A major share of the effort remained on national defense and security even after the first civilian reactors opened in the 1950s. That decade was marked by the fear that countries hostile to us—in particular, the Soviet Union —would develop nuclear weapons of their own and pose a threat to our national security. The feeling was that, to survive, we had to stay ahead of them in the development of nuclear weaponry. Again, the wastes went ignored.

The remarks of two experts clearly reveal the early attitude towards nuclear wastes. Dr. Edward Teller, the Hungarian-born physicist who became known as "the father of the hydrogen bomb," said that the disposal of the wastes did not constitute a scientific problem. He felt it was, instead, a political problem, meaning that it was one best handled by local, state, and federal authorities. Dr. Teller's view was generally accepted by the scientific community and can leave little doubt that science understood neither the dangers of the wastes nor the immediate need to beware of them.

Another revealing comment about our early attitudes about nuclear waste disposal was made in 1986, when the nation learned that the giant defense nuclear plant at Hanford, Washington, had for years disposed of some of its wastes by releasing them into the atmosphere, possibly damaging the health of residents of the area. The manager of the plant said that in light of today's knowledge the amounts released are regarded as very high, but that in earlier times they were not viewed as amounts that would have "dire consequences" for the people living near the plant. There will be more about the Hanford wastes later in this chapter.

Even more telling was the amount of money spent by the federal government on nuclear development in the 1950s and 1960s. Billions of dollars went into the development of both defense and civilian nuclear power. But only $300 million was assigned to researches into high-level wastes, their dangers, and the need to shield them.

Because of such thoughtlessness, the United States early established a tradition for the unsafe disposal of its civilian and military wastes that was to persist for years. In the eyes of many concerned citizens, the tradition continues at a number of nuclear sites to this day—long after the dangers of the wastes have become fully recognized. They feel that a number of factors, among them carelessness, have replaced the ignorance. We will see why as we go along.

STRANGE AND TRAGIC INCIDENTS

The early ignorance led to a number of strange and, at times, tragic incidents in later years. Here are just three examples.

The Day the Ground Crackled

A few years ago, some workers were clearing a vacant lot in the town of Parkersburg, West Virginia.[2] Suddenly, the ground underfoot began to crackle. Heat and flames erupted from the soil and set a bulldozer on fire.

The workers—and all the residents of Parkersburg —were startled to learn that the bulldozer had unearthed a shallow burial site for nuclear wastes that had been dumped there years before by a nearby defense nuclear plant and then had been forgotten.

The nation's press, in reporting the incident, remarked that the case was not an isolated one. The United States was said to be dotted with hundreds of vacant lots, wooded parks, and open areas that industries once used as "cemeteries" for their nuclear wastes.

The Hanford Drama

In early 1986, the government nuclear plant at Hanford, Washington, earned headlines across the nation when an environmental group reported that the installation had been disposing of its waste materials for years by releasing them into the atmosphere.[3] The group—the Hanford Education League, with headquarters in Spokane—based its report on secret U.S. government documents it had secured under the recently enacted Freedom of Information Act. The documents revealed that the plant had loosed great amounts of such dangerous radioactive wastes as iodine, ruthenium, and cesium in clouds of gases that had rolled out for miles from the plant.

Of particular concern was the vast amount of radioiodine that had been set free. Some 530,000 curies of the substance had been released over the years and ranked as the greatest amount ever discharged by a U.S. nuclear operation. Radioiodine is known for its power to penetrate the walls of body cells and cause healthy tissue to become diseased. It particularly affects the thyroid gland, which regulates our metabolism. It is also especially dangerous to children who are 100 times more susceptible than adults to its attacks.

Did fallout from the clouds of iodine and other radioactive wastes harm the surrounding area? For the people living there and for many scientists, the answer is a resounding "yes." Other scientists doubt that the harm, if any, was great.

The people in the small farming town of Mesa, which lies about ten miles east of the Hanford installation, are convinced that they suffered much harm. For example, one farmer, his wife, and three of their daughters all take medication for thyroid problems. Another resident reports that his father has colon cancer and his mother skin cancer. His two sisters have had their lower colons removed. The man says that he himself is sterile and has only 90 percent of his lung capacity. Over the years, small towns nearby also have reported an increase in thyroid problems—many of which have required removal of the gland.

Just outside Mesa is a rural area that has won the ugly nickname "the death mile." Of the 108 people who lived there while the clouds of gases were rolling in from the Hanford chimneys, 24 have become ill with or have died of cancer since the 1960s. Residents of the area report that seven children died in infancy or suffered physical handicaps.

Also feared are the 200 billion gallons of radioactive waste water that the Hanford plant poured into ponds and pits over the years. The concern here centers on whether or not the waste water, which resulted

Smoke billows out of the huge plutonium-producing plant in Hanford, Washington. The plant spreads over an area half the size of Rhode Island.

from the reprocessing of spent fuels, has filtered down to contaminate the area's underground water supply. In late 1988, *Time* magazine estimated that the amount of Hanford's dumped water was sufficient to create a lake some 40 feet deep and of a size to cover New York City's Manhattan.

But what of those scientists who believe that the unleashed wastes did little or no harm? Officials and scientists with the Department of Energy agree that the reports of illness are "compelling," but point out that there is as yet no scientific proof that the problems were triggered by the wastes. The belief is that the radioactive clouds were dispersed over such a wide area that their radioactivity was greatly diluted and that the doses of radiation reaching surrounding residents were probably too small to have caused significant harm.

This belief is greeted with widespread skepticism because it is voiced by officials of the U.S. government. The feeling is that the officials have a vested interest in protecting the reputation of a government facility.

The views of the DOE have been given some support, however, by a 1985 study conducted by a Washington state epidemiologist. The study indicated that the cancer death rate in the areas closest to Hanford is lower than the national average. The study was based on a survey of death records in two lightly populated regions close to the Hanford installation. The report has been criticized by local residents because it did not include the hard-hit "death mile" area.

Despite the contention that the gas clouds did little or no damage, the DOE in late 1988 launched a $15 million study to ascertain the directions taken by the clouds and to see how much radiation—especially the dreaded iodine radiation—might have been absorbed by people when consuming the area's water, milk, vegetables, and other foodstuffs. At the same time, the Federal Centers for Disease Control (headquartered in Atlanta, Georgia) began planning a five-year study of the people living near the Hanford plant to learn how they may have been affected by the discharged iodine. Some researchers already estimate that perhaps 20,000 children in the area may have been exposed to unhealthy levels of iodine by drinking the milk of cows that grazed on contaminated grasslands.

A Grim Surprise

In 1984, the people of Fernald, a town about eighteen miles outside Cincinnati, Ohio, were both puzzled and shocked to learn that their local animal feed plant was releasing uranium dust into the atmosphere.[4] Puzzled over why a feed plant was using uranium, they were shocked to learn that the plant was not producing feed at all, and had not done so in the more than thirty years since it opened in 1951.

Operating under the innocent name, Feed Materials Production Center, it was actually a top-secret defense plant that refined uranium to be used in the manufacture of warheads for intercontinental ballistic missiles (ICBMs) and other nuclear weapons. Though owned by the government, the plant was run by a company called National Lead of Ohio.

Fernald's shock turned to ugly fear when the people learned that their "feed" plant had been leaking uranium dust into the air since its opening and that the released amounts added up to thousands of pounds. During a 1988 congressional investigation of the plant, Dr. Richard Shank, director of Ohio's Environmental Protection Agency, testified that the plant had discharged about 298,000 pounds of uranium into the air over the years. Another 167,000 pounds had been discharged into the nearby Great Miami River.

Health officials said that uranium dust emitted a low-level radiation that was not dangerous outside the body. It could be lethal, however, if inhaled; it could penetrate the cells around the lungs, upset the body's biochemical processes, and possibly cause cancer. It could do the same harm in drinking water.

Then came the frightening disclosure that the plant also maintained one of the most dangerous nuclear waste dumps in the United States. The storage pits at the dump were described as old and leaky. Waste water had seeped from them and had channeled into Fernald's underground water supply and drinking-water wells. It had entered the Great Miami River, often pouring in when rains caused the pits to overflow. According to Dr. Shank's later congressional testimony, more than 12.5 million pounds of uranium had been stored in the pits since the plant's opening.

During an interview conducted in 1987 on the American Broadcasting Company's news program, "20/20," an official of the Sierra Club, a national environmental organization, charged that some 11 million pounds of the waste water were filtering deep into the ground and leaking into the Grant-Miami aquifer, the largest source of underground water in the Midwest.

Several environmentalists and Fernald residents were interviewed on the program. They accused the plant of using old and faulty equipment. They also charged that, as early as 1960, plant officials knew that the dump pits might be leaking waste into the surrounding underground water supply but did nothing about the problem.

These charges pointed to the ignorance of earlier years and also provided examples of the kinds of carelessness that were seen later at a number of nuclear sites. One environmentalist quoted from reports that described the plant's equipment and technology as being poor even at the time of its construction. A former plant employee claimed that 50 percent of the installation's maintenance procedures had not been revised or reviewed since 1960.

The Fernald situation saw the Department of Energy accused of ignoring federal safety regulations for the operation of nuclear plants and the disposal of their wastes. During the 1988 congressional investigation, DOE officials admitted that the federal government had long known of the plant's deficiencies but had decided not to spend the money necessary to correct them. Estimates of the cost of renovating the plant's equipment and cleaning up the waste problem had run between $450 million and $600 million.

The DOE is presently working on a study, requested by Ohio Senator John Glenn, to determine whether the massive amounts of released uranium caused surrounding residents to be exposed to excessive radiation levels. Upon receiving the study results, the Centers for Disease Control are to estimate the radiation dosages received by the residents and then decide whether they were high enough to require a health survey of the area.

THE BLINDNESS ENDS

By the 1970s, an increasing number of federal regulations governing nuclear plant and waste safety had gone into effect. They were developed first by the Atomic Energy Commission (the nation's first nuclear governing body) and then by its successor, the Department of Energy.

By this time, the nation's civilian and defense nuclear operations had begun to learn the need for the careful storage of their high-level and low-level wastes. Systems of storage were developed that remain in use today.[5]

HLW and LLW Storage Today
Commercial spent fuel assemblies (as you know, a major example of high-level waste) are shielded from their surroundings by immersion in water-filled tanks, called "ponds," at the nuclear power plants; water, remember, is one of the dense materials that satisfactorily shields HLW radiation. Government HLWs are stored principally in underground steel tanks on selected federal lands.

Government low-level wastes are likewise stored on selected federal lands; shallow burial is the system used. Commercial LLWs are buried at power plant sites or at commercially operated dumps that have been established for this express purpose.

Both the 1960s and 1970s saw the establishment of the commercially operated dumps, six in all. Actually, only one of them—located at Beatty, Nevada—was opened in the 1960s. The rest were set up during the 1970s at Hanford, Washington; Barnwell, South Carolina; West Valley, New York; Maxey Flats, Kentucky; and Sheffield, Illinois. Because of various problems, the West Valley, Maxey Flats, and Sheffield sites were short-lived; they were closed by the end of the decade. The Hanford, Barnwell, and Beatty dumps are the only depositories for civilian LLWs in the country at present.

Temporary Systems

The present storage systems for the high- and low-level wastes are temporary. They are being used as interim solutions to the storage problem while plans are being developed for the permanent storage installations that the most potent and long-lived of the wastes require. The current facilities are considered temporary for several reasons. Some are not large enough to handle all the future waste accumulations. Some are not geologically suitable for centuries of storage. And some are not in the best locations for long-term storage.

What kinds of plans are under way for the permanent storage of the wastes? The answer begins with two pieces of legislation passed by the U.S. Congress during the early 1980s: the Low-Level Radioactive Waste Policy Act (1980) and the Nuclear Waste Policy Act (1982). The former deals with commercial LLWs. The latter concerns all high-level wastes generated by commercial or defense operations; it also covers the LLWs created by defense work.

We turn now to these acts for a look at what they hold for the future.

4

STORING THE
LOW-LEVEL WASTES

The Low-Level Radioactive Waste Policy Act of 1980 established two national policies for the permanent disposal of LLWs. The policies apply to the wastes generated by the commercial nuclear operations in the various states.[1]

First, the act stipulates that each state is responsible for disposing of the LLWs generated by its own commercial reactors and other nuclear activities, such as medical research and treatment. On the other hand, no state is held accountable for its commercial high-level wastes; nor is it responsible for the high- and low-level wastes generated by defense work within its borders. The job of getting rid of those wastes falls to the U.S. government.

Second, the act calls for neighboring states to join together in regional groups, called compacts. Each compact is to fashion agreements for developing permanent disposal methods and facilities that are best suited to its needs. A chief aim here is to keep the number of dump sites at a reasonable total. Some thirty states currently maintain commercial nuclear power plants. The U.S. map in Figure 4 shows where nuclear reactors with on-site radioactive storages are located. It also indicates those states which produce spent nuclear fuel and high-level wastes and those states expected to generate waste by the year 2000.

The plants vary in number from state to state— some states have only one, others have several (six or more in some cases). But let us imagine that each of the forty-eight continental states maintained at least one plant and adjoining disposal site. The nation would be dotted with a minimum of forty-eight sites. However, if compacts of, say, six states each were formed and then one site was chosen to serve all six, the number of sites would drop to eight. (Hawaii and Alaska would probably require their own disposal installations because they are too distant from their fellow states to share facilities with them.)

Further, some states do not have the remote and sparsely populated areas best suited for safe disposal, while others do. Regional compacts give the states the best chance of finding the most suitable locations.

The Low-Level Radioactive Waste Policy Act, though widely viewed as a sensible way for the states to handle the permanent storage of their LLWs, has caused an assortment of problems, not least of which is the need to select the best and safest disposal method. The problem is complicated by the fact that the wastes come in both liquid and solid forms. Each form demands a disposal system of its own.

LIQUID LOW-LEVEL
WASTE DISPOSAL

Though much of the liquid waste emerges from the defense reprocessing of spent fuels to recycle their ura-

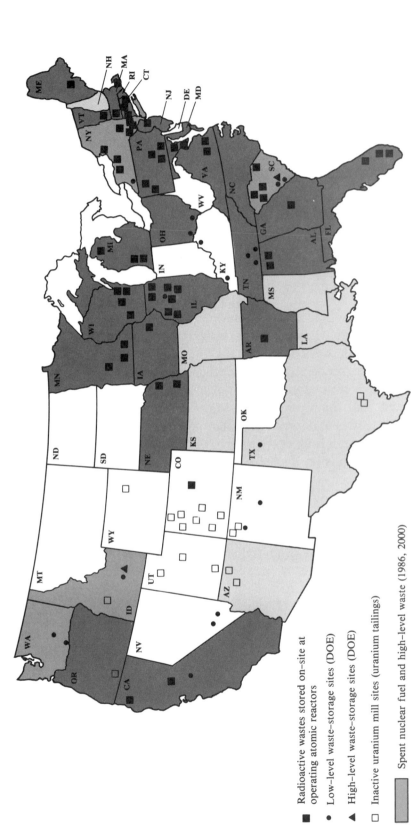

■ Radioactive wastes stored on-site at operating atomic reactors

● Low-level waste–storage sites (DOE)

▲ High-level waste–storage sites (DOE)

□ Inactive uranium mill sites (uranium tailings)

Spent nuclear fuel and high-level waste (1986, 2000)

Spent nuclear fuel only (1986)

Additional states with spent nuclear fuel by the year 2000

Sources: Office of Civilian Radioactive Waste Management (DOE) and Radioactive Waste Campaign Inc.

Figure 4. Radioactive Storage Sites and States with Existing and Projected Inventories of Spent Nuclear Fuel and High–Level Waste

nium and plutonium, some liquid LLW is generated by civilian reactors and other facilities. The disposal of liquid LLW involves several problems. They can be seen by examining the three systems that have been used to dispose of it over the years. There are: ground percolation, deep well injection, and grout injection.[2]

Ground Percolation

In ground percolation, the liquid LLW is directed to open ponds or underground cribs. It is then allowed to seep down through soil, sand, and gravel to underground water sources at a depth of about 100 meters.

This method was employed in the early years of the nuclear era when scientists believed that the wastes, with their weak and usually short-lived radiation, would be rendered harmless when diluted in the vast expanses of underground water. It is now known, however, that the stronger and more durable LLWs can pollute the underground water and the surrounding subterranean rock and soil formations. Hence, ground percolation is no longer used in the United States—or in a number of foreign countries—and is not seen as a feasible disposal system for the future.

Deep Well Injection

The idea behind deep well injection is to mimic nature's way of storing petroleum, gas, and water, all of which have been locked in natural traps within the earth for millions of years. Boreholes are drilled to fissures and caverns deep within the earth's crust and the liquid LLW is then sent downward to occupy those spaces.

Deep well injection has a major drawback. Through the years, much LLW has been stored at power plant and reprocessing sites. The geologic strata beneath many of the installations have proved unsuitable because they are without fissures and caverns adequate for the process. Consequently, deep well injection is little used today and, unless some of the compacts can find the proper geologic formations, it will likely go ignored in the future.

Grout Injection
Grout injection is similar to deep well injection, but involves an extra step. When the liquid LLW is injected into the ground, it is accompanied by grout, which is a plasterlike substance. Once underground, the grout solidifies and locks in the waste's radiation.

Grout injection holds the promise of being an effective system for the state compacts. It has been in general use for some years at the federal government's Oak Ridge Laboratory in Tennessee. It is being considered for use in at least one foreign country, West Germany.

SOLID LOW-LEVEL
WASTE DISPOSAL

Liquids, of course, make up only a portion of the low-level wastes. There are also all those various solid objects that have been rendered radioactive and hence too dangerous for future use—everything from clothing to research laboratory gear. Swelling the list are the liquid wastes that have been solidified by allowing their water content to evaporate.

Two methods have been used through the years to dispose of the solid wastes: controlled sea dumping and shallow land burial. A third method being considered for future use is burial in mined cavities.

Controlled Sea Dumping

Beginning in the late 1940s, solid LLWs were packaged in 55-gallon to 80-gallon steel drums and dumped into the sea from ships and aircraft operating off both the Atlantic and Pacific coasts.[3] The drums were lined to 75 percent of capacity with concrete. The concrete served two purposes. It was intended to be a protective measure against radiation leakage and a means of weighting the drums so that they would sink to a depth of some 12,000 feet.

Only wastes from defense plants were involved during the late 1940s and early 1950s because the nation had yet to build its first commercial reactor. Their dumping immediately presented two problems. First, as an understanding of the dangers of the wastes began to dawn, the order went out to deposit the LLWs only in designated areas selected for their depths distance from commercial fishing grounds. Unfortunately, however, these designated drop-off points often were ignored by the waste-carrying ships and planes. Sometimes bad weather prevented an aircraft from reaching the designated spot before running low on fuel. Sometimes, aircraft or ship crews simply wanted to save time so that they could get home at a reasonable hour. The captains of commercial ships under contract to the government often returned to shore quickly so that they would not have to pay their crews overtime wages. In such cases, the drums would be "short dumped"—dropped in any convenient spot, regardless of its depth or its proximity to a fishing ground.

The second problem came to light soon after sea dumping began. Many of the drums were not sufficiently weighted and failed to sink. They floated on the surface and, when sighted, were not picked up for proper repackaging but were split open and sunk by naval gunfire. Their radioactive contents spilled into the ocean to pollute the waters and endanger the surrounding sea life.

In light of today's knowledge, "short dumping" and the practice of sinking the drums by gunfire seem inexcusable. But again it must be remembered that an understanding of the LLW dangers was limited during those early years. It was believed that the oceans were so vast that the waste would be dispersed and diluted enough to make it harmless. We now know that while some of the waste is rendered harmless, much of it sticks to the sea bottom and lies there as a constant threat to the surrounding marine life—and a threat to anyone who eats contaminated fish.

Government officials estimate that over the years some 90,000 waste-filled drums were dropped in the Pacific off the coast of California, and in the Atlantic from Massachusetts south to the Carolinas. It is also estimated that at least several thousand of them have broken open and spread their radioactivity over the surrounding sea bottom. It would be impossible to retrieve the drums because storms and sea tides have altered the ocean floor over the years, burying many of the drums and shifting some to other locations. Also, the unauthorized areas where many were dumped are unknown.

In 1970, the administration of President Richard M. Nixon banned the sea dumping of government wastes in an attempt to curb the damage; at present, they are stored on selected federal lands. Unfortunately, the Nixon ban did not end *all* sea dumping. By 1970, the Atlantic and Pacific oceans (and some of the nation's lakes) were being used as disposal sites for commercial solid low-level wastes, especially the wastes produced by nuclear medicine. Commercial dumping led to a number of incidents that infuriated the nation in the 1980s.[4]

Commercial services working under contract to medical organizations customarily dumped such radioactive garbage as broken syringes, empty drug vials, toweling, and rubber gloves. The wastes began washing up along Florida's Gulf of Mexico shoreline. The same thing happened on two Ohio beaches that fronted Lake Erie. Then the coasts of the states of New York and New Jersey were befouled with medical wastes and raw sewage that floated ashore during the summer of 1988.

Governors Mario M. Cuomo of New York and Thomas H. Kean of New Jersey took quick action on behalf of their states. They instituted regulations that would demand a "cradle-to-grave" accounting of all hazardous medical wastes. The regulations called for waste to be tracked from its inception to its disposal. Records would be kept on the creation of the waste at a medical facility, then on its transportation to a disposal spot, and finally on the location of its ultimate disposal.

Governor Cuomo announced that the purpose of the regulations is to warn the dumpers that "we will watch you with the intent of catching and prosecuting you if this waste is not disposed of properly." Governor Kean said, "We will no longer tolerate the careless, unsupervised, and often just outrageous way these wastes are being handled."

In early August 1988, the federal government joined the two states in the campaign against nuclear medical waste. The U.S. Congress enacted the Medical Tracking Law, which made ocean dumping of medical wastes a federal offense.

The United States is not alone in creating environmental problems by dumping nuclear wastes at sea. Great Britain generated havoc in the Irish Sea by discharging tons of high-level wastes—deadly plutonium, ruthenium, and cesium-137 among them—into its waters. News reports hold that the British government's power plant and reprocessing center at Sellafield has leaked a quarter-ton of plutonium into the Irish Sea over a thirty-five-year period.

Marilynne Robinson, in her book *Mother Country,* calls Great Britain the world's largest producer of plutonium and the greatest dumper of radioactive waste on the environment. She accuses the country of being responsible for 90 percent of the nuclear waste found in the world's seas. In reporting on the harm done by the Sellafield plant, Ms. Robinson writes that the fish in the Irish Sea are 5,000 times more radioactive than those in the North Sea (which, she says, has also been contaminated) and that lambs and produce grown in the Sellafield area are laced with radioactivity. She goes on to report that the incidence of childhood leukemia in the Sellafield area is ten times Great Britain's national average.

Shallow Land Burial

Shallow land burial is the system currently employed for the temporary storage of commercial and government solid LLWs in the United States.[5] Shallow burial, which calls for wastes to be deposited in trenches that are capped with soil or concrete when full, has long been practiced in the United States and elsewhere. It was first tried by the United States—with unhappy results—during World War II.

The first shallow burials were made in 1943 by workers on the Manhattan Project (the program that

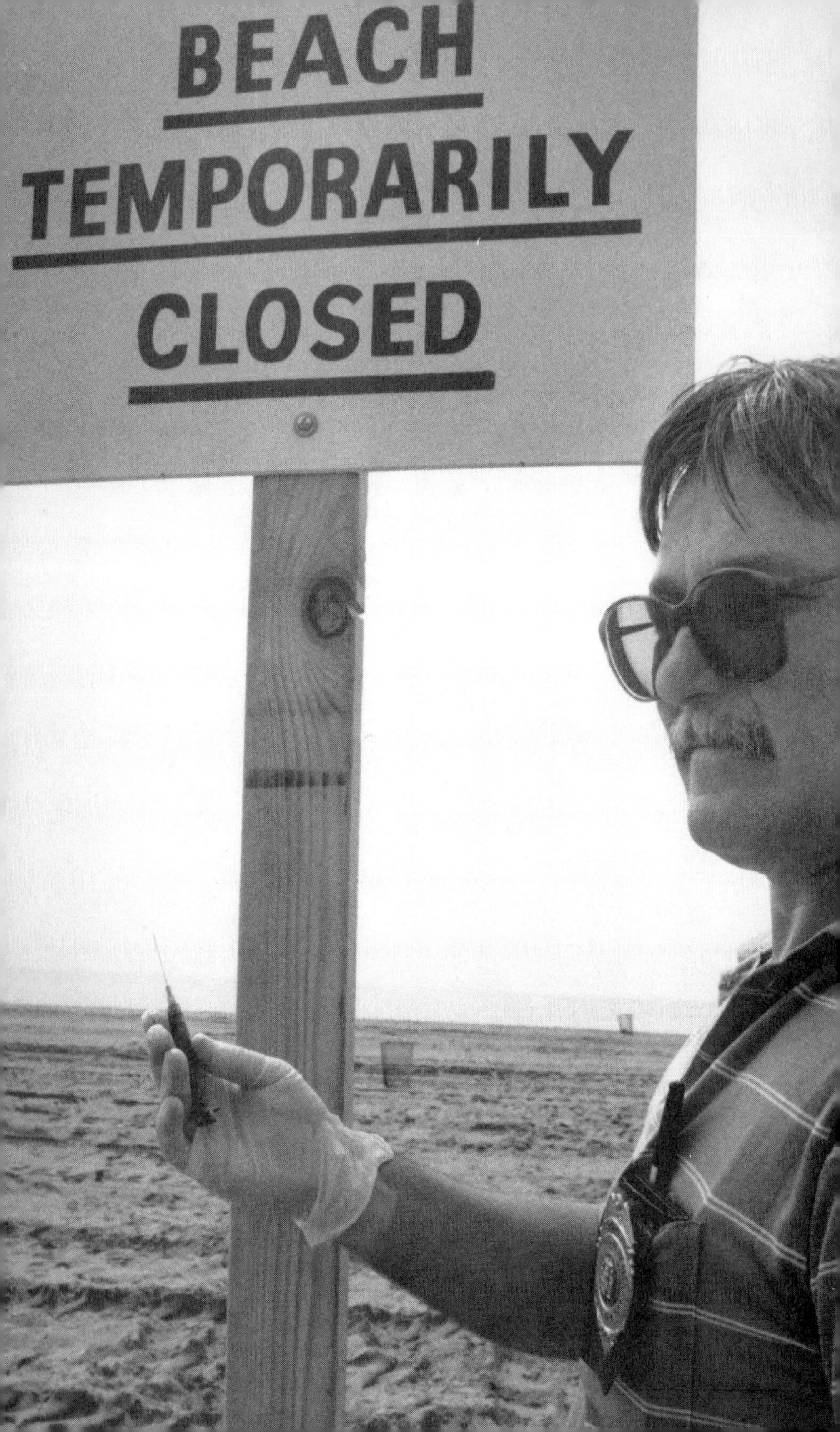
BEACH
TEMPORARILY
CLOSED

developed the atomic bomb). The wastes were generated by a reactor in Chicago and dumped into trenches two feet deep at Palos Forest, a park preserve just twenty miles outside the city, and later covered over with concrete. In the years since, the wastes have contaminated nearby underground and well water. They have also spread high concentrations of uranium and plutonium to adjoining meadows. Today, the dump site is marked with a stone tablet that warns visitors: "Caution. Do Not Dig." Palos Forest continues to be a popular spot for hikers, picnickers, and campers. The site is scheduled for a clean-up by the federal government.

The trenches give mute evidence of how little the dangers of the wastes were understood in 1943—and of how concentration on development of the atom bomb left little or no time to think about their possible harm.

Through the years, the techniques of shallow burial have been improved. Today, the trenches are lined with concrete. They contain special backfill materials. The adjacent ground is fitted with drainage systems to prevent rainwater from eroding their sides and tops. Their locations are chosen according to scientific guidelines. The wastes that go into them are often locked in steel containers.

It is likely that shallow burial or a similar system—burial in mined cavities—will be the choice of many state compacts.

An inspector from the New York City Department of Health holds up a used syringe that washed up along with other kinds of medical waste on Staten Island's South Beach.

Burial in Mined Cavities

Burial in mined cavities is also known as geologic burial.[6] It calls for solid LLWs to be placed in natural caves or in underground caverns built especially for storage purposes. Prior to burial, the wastes are encased in steel canisters. The caves and caverns are sealed when finally filled to capacity.

SETTING UP THE COMPACTS

A number of states have already reached agreements to form compacts.[7] For example:

- Northwest: Alaska, Idaho, Montana, Oregon, Utah, Washington. Hawaii is also a member of this compact.

- West: California and Arizona.

- Rocky Mountain Region: Colorado, New Mexico, Nevada, Wyoming.

- Midwest: Iowa, Indiana, Michigan, Minnesota, Missouri, Ohio, Wisconsin. Another midwestern compact has linked Illinois with Kentucky.

- Southeast: Alabama, Florida, Georgia, Mississippi, North Carolina, South Carolina, Tennessee, Virginia.

At least one state, Texas, has chosen to operate on its own. Some other states are considering the formation of compacts. Still others—especially those with no nuclear plants and no plans to build any—are undecided as to whether it will be necessary or advisable to join a compact.

Along with the need to choose the best permanent storage system possible, the compacts will be faced with a string of other knotty problems. Questions such as the following will have to be answered:

- Should we use any of the already-established disposal sites within our compact or decide on a new one?* Are the current sites suitable for permanent storage? Or large enough to handle the amount of waste that will be brought in from the entire compact? If they do not meet our needs, where will we find a spot that does?

- When we do select a site, will it be agreeable to everyone? What if it lies within a state that produces little waste? Will the people there object to seeing their state become the dumping ground for states that generate great amounts of waste? How can a spot agreeable to the majority of people be found?

- Will people everywhere in our compact object to having the roads near them used to transport the wastes to the storage site? How fearful will they be of roadway mishaps that might unleash poisonous radiation? To ease these fears and insure public safety, how must we package the wastes so that their radioactivity will not escape in the event of an accident? What kind of

* In at least two instances, this question has already been resolved. California plans to provide the disposal sites in its compact with Arizona. Illinois intends doing the same with Kentucky. Both California and Illinois are major producers of nuclear energy. Arizona and Kentucky are not.

regulations will we need to make certain that the wastes are always carefully and safely transported?

The states are now working on the answers to these questions. Washington, D.C. is facing the same questions as, under the Nuclear Waste Policy Act of 1982, it develops plans for the permanent storage of the nation's commercial and government high-level wastes. In the next chapters, we will see that the federal government has come up with some answers. They are answers that may prove helpful to the state compacts.

5

CORROSION, LEAKS, AND IDEAS

As you know, the present systems for the storage of high-level wastes are considered temporary for several reasons. Some are not geologically suitable for the centuries of shielding the HLWs require. Others are not large enough to accommodate all the liquid and solid matter that will accumulate in the future. Some are not in the best locations for long-term storage.

In passing the Nuclear Waste Policy Act, Congress ordered the Department of Energy to develop a facility for the permanent storage of the wastes. To understand the factors that led to this order, we need to look briefly at the story of HLW storage to date and the problems it has encountered over the years.

TEMPORARY HIGH-LEVEL STORAGE

The dangers of potent HLWs were the first to be recognized. They were a matter of growing concern for many scientists as far back as World War II. In the late

1940s and early 1950s, much of the worry centered on the fact that the HLWs, in both liquid and solid form, were accumulating at a disturbing rate as the United States worked to maintain a nuclear superiority over its adversaries by expanding its atomic research and production for defense purposes.

Once the liquid and solid HLWs were recognized as dangers, steps began to be taken for their careful storage. Since the solid wastes—which consisted mainly of spent fuel assemblies—could be safely stored in water-filled tanks at the nuclear plant sites, we will examine the problems caused by the liquid wastes that were emerging from the government reprocessing of spent fuels.

THE LIQUIDS: A TALE OF CORROSION AND LEAKAGE

The story of the liquids can begin at the government facility at Hanford, Washington.[1] Built in the 1940s, the plant did much early reprocessing work. It stored the resultant liquid HLWs in large underground tanks. The tanks were built of carbon steel and were of single-wall construction.

But there was trouble. The liquids were acidic. They threatened to corrode the tank walls and allow the wastes to escape and poison the surrounding ground. To side-step this threat, Hanford neutralized the acidity with sodium hydroxide. Though the method solved the corrosion problem, it created a new headache. The sodium hydroxide added to the volume of the waste and caused a sludge to form in the tanks. The plant intended to dispose of the wastes later by first solidifying them through the evaporation of their water content and then removing the solids from the tanks. But the sludge was going to make the removal especially difficult, if not impossible.

In the early 1950s double-wall tanks came into use as an extra safeguard against leaks caused by corrosion or other breaks in the tanks. Double-wall tanks were installed at the government facilities at Savannah River in North Carolina and Idaho Falls, Idaho. The Savannah River liquids were neutralized with sodium hydroxide and stored in carbon steel tanks. Idaho Falls did not at first neutralize its wastes but deposited them directly into stainless steel tanks.

In 1956, Hanford reported its first leaking tank. In the years that followed, adding to the problems caused by Hanford's emissions of radioactive waste into the atmosphere, some 450,000 gallons of high-level liquid waste seeped from 20 of the plant's 149 tanks. (The waste seems to have been successfully absorbed by the surrounding earth; as of the 1980s, there were no reports of serious underground water pollution caused by the leaks.) One of the Savannah River tanks began to leak in 1960. About 100 gallons of high-level waste escaped into the ground and contaminated a nearby source of underground water. The government has been much criticized for these and other leaks. It has responded by claiming that only a mere fraction—less than 1 percent—of all its stored liquid waste has escaped via leakage.

Two Government Moves
The leaks at Hanford—and elsewhere—caused the government to take two actions. First, during the 1960s, the Atomic Energy Commission (the organization that preceded the DOE as the agency in charge of the government's nuclear work) began calling for the

plants to solidify the wastes, a process that would end the danger of leakage and also reduce the volume of waste. In response, Hanford and Savannah River evaporated the water content of their neutralized wastes. Left behind in the tanks was a reduced mixture of liquid and sludges. At the Idaho Falls plant, where wastes had not been neutralized, they were chemically treated and turned into calcine, a dry granular material. The calcine was then transferred to stainless steel bins in concrete-lined underground chambers.

Second, during the 1970s, the government began giving greater attention to improving temporary storage facilities. Twenty-seven new tanks were constructed at Savannah River and twenty at Hanford. The new construction was intended to eliminate the single-wall tanks at both sites by transferring their liquid content to the new tanks. There was no problem with the transfer, but then a difficulty arose that stalled matters for years to come. Remaining in the old tanks were those sludges. They had to be dissolved and removed, a job that involved the use of nitric acid. The acid hastened the corrosion of the old tanks and threatened to release even more waste into the ground.

This picture shows one of the reactors at the Three Mile Island nuclear plant. A small, low-level radioactive leak in the cooling system of another reactor resulted in the shutdown and evacuation of the plant.

Current Work

At present, Hanford and Savannah River are researching ways to solve the leakage and sludge removal problems.[2] Savannah River has come up with a method for successfully ridding itself of the sludge. It is also installing a system for converting its liquid waste into a glass-like substance.

Plans at Hanford call for the different elements in its HLWs to be separated from each other. The highly radioactive portions are to be solidified and held for later permanent storage. The portions with lower radioactivity are to be injected into the earth along with the plaster-like substance, grout, which will then solidify and lock in their radiation.

Similar work is being done at the civilian reprocessing plant at West Valley, New York. The plant, which has been closed for many years, is presently being decontaminated, meaning that its radioactive materials and wastes are being cleaned up and removed from its various facilities. A ceramic melter will then be installed at the site. The melter will solidify the high-level radioactive waste and convert it into a glass-like form. The decontamination work is being done under a joint federal/state plan.

Constructed in the 1960s, West Valley was the first civilian installation for the reprocessing of spent fuels. It neutralized its liquid wastes and placed them underground in steel tanks. The tanks boasted an extra safety feature. Each had a giant saucer fitted beneath it to catch any leakage (a technique that was later used at Hanford). Throughout the six years of its operation, West Valley stored about 60,000 gallons of high-level wastes. The plant was closed in the early 1970s, in part because drainage problems caused some of its storage facilities to overflow and contaminate the surrounding area during rainstorms.

HLW PERMANENT STORAGE: IDEAS AND MORE IDEAS

By the 1980s, the leaks—and the mounting accumulation of solid HLWs at both defense and civilian nuclear plants—left no doubt that steps must be taken to establish a definite system for permanent storage. Thus the Nuclear Waste Policy Act came into being.

Prior to the act's passage, the DOE had been searching for a safe method of permanent disposal and had looked into six proposed methods. Each called for the wastes to be placed in sealed canisters for disposal.[3]

Subseabed Emplacement
As its name indicates, subseabed emplacement proposes that the wastes be deposited below the ocean floor in any of three locations. The first two are deep sea trenches and mid-oceanic fracture zones (areas where the ocean floor is split open). The third, which strikes many scientists as the best, is deep-sea layers of clay at the center of stable areas of the ocean floor.

The concept was considered workable, but it presented a number of practical difficulties that made the DOE reject it. (It is, however, as we will see later, being studied today for possible use by several nations.) For one thing, before the system could ever be attempted, it needed to be approved by an international agreement because the burial was to be carried out in international waters. For another, the process would require transporting the waste canisters over long distances; turbulent seas and hazardous weather could sink the transport ships and result in the contamination of such areas as coastal waters and commercial fishing grounds with radioactivity.

Extraterrestrial Disposal
The exact opposite of subseabed emplacement is extraterrestrial disposal. Instead of burying the waste canisters deep beneath the ocean floor, this plan would fire them into deep space and allow them to float there. Or it would store them aboard rockets that would then be launched toward the sun.

Extraterrestrial disposal was considered unworkable on two counts. First, there have long been angry and frightened objections worldwide at any mention of cluttering space with any kind of garbage. The nuclear variety stands at the head of the items that no one wants to see orbiting the earth. Second, the dangers that would accompany the launch of any space vehicle were made even more terrifying by adding the consequences of an accident to a rocket with radioactive cargo aboard.

Ice Sheet Emplacement
This idea of ice sheet emplacement is based on the fact that HLWs emit great heat. Waste canisters would be placed on the vast ice sheets that cover the island of Greenland and the continent of Antarctica. The heat radiating from the containers would melt the ice, enabling them to sink deep into it. When the ice cooled again, it would solidify around the canisters and lock in their radioactivity.

Actually, the DOE was presented with three different methods of ice sheet emplacement. The first, called passive slow descent, would insert the canisters in shallow holes and then allow them to sink until they reached the bottom of the ice sheet. The second, known as the anchor concept, is similar to passive descent, except that a cable attached to each canister would permit it to sink no farther than a designated level and would enable it to be retrieved at a later date in the event of an emergency.

The third method is known as surface emplacement. It involves constructing large storage units on the surface of the ice and filling them with the waste canisters. The heat radiated would cause the units to melt their way slowly to the bottom of the sheet.

The DOE could see several advantages to ice sheet emplacement. To begin, the burial would be made in remote and desolate regions (Antarctica was especially favored because it is uninhabited by humans) and thus place the wastes in almost total isolation. Next, the burial would be deep because the ice sheets are amazingly thick (the thickness of some ranging up to 10,000 feet or more). Further, they are formations that, unlike the earth, remain stable for long periods, insuring that the burial would not be disturbed by such upheavals as earthquakes.

But there were also several drawbacks to the concept that led to its rejection by the DOE. There were the usual hazards inherent in transporting the wastes over great distances to the disposal sites; the hazards seemed especially ominous because the transport ships would be sailing into the world's worst weather. Furthermore, the bitter polar cold, and the long periods of polar darkness, guaranteed that the work of burial would be particularly difficult and dangerous. Perhaps the greatest drawback of all was that the United States, along with a number of other nations, had signed the Antarctic Treaty of 1959. The treaty specifically prohibits the disposal of nuclear waste on the continent at the bottom of the world.

Island Disposal

Like the process of burial in mined cavities (described in Chapter Four), island disposal is a system of geologic burial. In geologic burial, the wastes are interred not in masses of ice but in natural or man-made caverns lying beneath the earth's surface. This particular type of geologic burial recommends that the burial take place on uninhabited islands far from civilization. It offers several advantages. Because the islands are uninhabited, the danger to health from radioactivity leaking into the atmosphere would be nil. Along the same line, any leakage into the island's underground water would also do no one any harm.

But the DOE saw two disadvantages in the system. The first was the obvious danger involved in shipping the wastes to distant burial sites. The second was that many islands are prone to intense seismic and volcanic disturbances. An earthquake or exploding volcano could rupture the canisters and discharge enough radioactivity into the atmosphere to threaten distant inhabited locales.

Deep Underground Melting

Deep underground melting is another system of geologic burial. Like ice sheet emplacement, it is based on the fact that HLWs give off great heat. It requires drilling holes down to fissures and cavities deep within the earth and then placing the wastes there. Once the water in the wastes has evaporated and converted them into solids, they will emit such an intense heat that the surrounding rock formations will melt. The melting will create a sphere of molten material that will eventually begin to cool and solidify. The result will be a solid mass of waste and rock in which the radioactive elements are trapped.

Deep underground melting contained a flaw that caused the DOE to eventually put it aside. The rock would need an excessively long time to solidify and seal in the radioactivity—sometimes a thousand years or more. In that time, too many things could happen below the earth's surface that might render the method unsafe.

Burial in Deep-Mined Cavities
Still another system of geologic burial, this plan entails disposing of the HLWs by interring them in deep-mined cavities. It proposes that a complex network of tunnels be constructed approximately six miles beneath the earth's surface. The tunnel floors would then be fitted with shallow holes into which the waste canisters would be inserted to keep them securely in place. To insure that the canisters would not bump against each other during any shifts of the surrounding geologic formations, the spaces between them would be covered with thick layers of dirt. Once filled to capacity with containers, the tunnels would be completely sealed off.

Because maximum isolation was provided for the wastes, the DOE subjected the plan to serious research for a time, but finally turned it down. The drilling of holes to a depth of six miles and then the construction of tunnels at that depth were deemed impossible. Additionally, no one knew how the rock at that depth would withstand any geologic upheavals or the intense heat emitted by the HLWs.

Although the concept of burial in deep-mined cavities was rejected, it did point the way to the system that Congress finally decided should be used for the permanent storage of high-level wastes. That system was specified in the Nuclear Waste Policy Act. We turn now to the act to examine the system and how the government plans to put it to use.

6

AN ACT AND
A SEARCH

In the Nuclear Waste Policy Act, Congress dictated that a system of geologic burial be used for the permanent storage of the nation's commercial and government high-level wastes. It ordered a system that resembled two of the disposal methods that we have discussed—burial in mined cavities for low-level wastes and burial in deep-mined cavities for HLWs. But there were differences.

The new system called for the construction of what would be known as an underground repository, a complex network of tunnels in which the wastes would be placed. The difference was that the burial would be deeper than needed for the low-level wastes but not as deep as deep-mined burial.

THE NUCLEAR WASTE
POLICY ACT: SPECIFICS

In addition to settling on geologic burial as the system of choice, the act contained a number of specific points.[1] For example, the measure:

- Told the Department of Energy to find an appropriate location for the repository and then to design, build, and operate the facility.

- Ordered the DOE to have the repository ready to begin accepting wastes for permanent storage by January 31, 1998.

- Directed the DOE to find a site for a second repository to be used at some unspecified future date.

- Instructed the DOE to work with civilian utilities to help them provide for the safe storage of their high-level wastes until the wastes could be moved to the permanent storage site. (This provision was placed in the Act because the planned repository was to handle commercial as well as government wastes. Under the provision, utility companies that provide their customers with nuclear generated power were to pay the federal government one mill—a tenth of a cent—per kilowatt hour of power created through nuclear means. This charge would be passed on to customers via increases in their monthly bills. It is currently being collected and brings in a total of about $500 million per year.)

Estimates held that the entire cost of establishing the facility and putting it in operation would cost between $21 and $42 billion.

The act also granted certain rights to the states and the nation's Indian tribes.[2] It awarded them the right to have independent checks and tests made of the DOE's investigation into any of their lands as a possible repository site. Further, if state or Indian land is selected for use, both have the right to study the plans being made for the construction and operation of the installation and, if necessary, to challenge them and work for their change. The act then stipulated that the state and tribes be given financial assistance to cover the costs entailed in their efforts.

These rights were granted to the Indian tribes largely because of the American Indian Religious Freedom Act of 1978, which bars the federal government from interfering with the rights of Indians to practice their religious beliefs. It states that American Indians must always have access to their sacred grounds and objects. Because land and nature are basic to a native American's religious worship, care must be taken that neither is violated by the repository planning and construction.

Though the DOE was shouldered with the responsibility of finding a site and then building and operating the repository, the act called for several other government agencies to assist with the project.[3] The Nuclear Regulatory Commission, which oversees the nation's commercial production of nuclear energy has the task of granting the DOE a license to build the repository. The license is to be awarded on the basis of standards that the commission develops to govern both the construction and subsequent operation of the facility. The commission is involved because the installation will store commercial as well as government wastes.

The Environmental Protection Agency, which safeguards the nation's environment, is to establish standards that will protect the public from the hazards that accompany the storing of the wastes. The act also

THIS UNSPOILED LAND
IS BEING CONSIDERED FOR A
NUCLEAR WASTE
REPOSITORY
BY U.S. DEPT OF ENERGY

directed the Department of Transportation to develop regulations and methods for the safe shipment of the wastes to the repository.

The Department of Justice is to give whatever legal assistance is needed; the Department of Defense is to acquire the land finally selected for the repository; the Department of Agriculture is to help with studies concerning the social and economic effects of the repository on any area where a site is under consideration; and the Department of the Interior is to provide several services, among them the mapping of any proposed sites located on lands under its control.

Finally, the act established a special department—the Office of Civilian Radioactive Waste Management (OCRWM)—within the DOE. It holds the responsibility for managing the repository program and seeing that the terms of the act are carried out.

THE STORAGE FACILITY

What kind of repository does the Department of Energy intend to build?[4] The proposed installation will resemble a large mining complex. There will be buildings at ground level for various uses. Below the surface, at a depth of 1,000 feet, will be the storage tunnels. Into them—there to remain for thousands of

The federal government is considering several sites for the final disposal of nuclear waste, including this area near Canyonlands National Park in Utah.

years—will go canisters filled with waste and sealed to prevent the escape of radiation. Until the repository is filled to capacity, it will be possible to retrieve the containers and haul them up to the surface if they are needed for some reason. When the repository reaches capacity, it will be filled with dirt and sealed off. The underground workings are planned to spread out over 1,500 acres.

The area at ground level is expected to cover from 150 to 400 acres. A series of ramps and shafts will link the surface facilities to the underground operation. The principal ground-level building will be the waste-handling plant. Here, the incoming waste will be received and given the final preparation necessary for burial.

Other ground-level facilities will include rail and truck unloading areas, warehouses, administration buildings, water and sewage treatment plants, a security office, and an area for holding the rock excavated in the construction or extension of the underground tunnels and chambers.

To ensure that the entire operation is secure from accidental intrusions by the public, an area three miles wide will surround the storage site. This area will be controlled by the installation's security force.

THE SEARCH FOR
A SITE

Under the terms of the act, the DOE's first job was to find a location suitable for the depository.[5] Once the spot was located, the department would recommend it to the president, who would then pass the matter on to Congress for consideration. Simultaneously, the state in which the site lay—plus any Indian tribes that might be affected by the repository—would have the right to disapprove the recommendation. Should either or both do so, Congress would be able to override the objections and proceed with the site or order the DOE to find another. Should all parties concerned—the Congress, the state, and the tribes—give their approval, the DOE would then apply to the Nuclear Regulatory Commission for a license to build the repository.

Actually, the DOE set about looking for two sites —the one that was needed immediately and one to be used at an unspecified date in the future. The department planned to have one serve the nuclear operations in the eastern half of the nation, and the other for those in the West. It was felt that the two widely separated locations would provide the best service by reducing the number of miles that the wastes would have to travel en route to final storage.

The DOE hoped to find a geological stability of the kind seen at Gabon on the Atlantic coast of central Africa. There, some 2 billion years ago, nature caused a rich uranium deposit to undergo a nuclear fission. The same types of waste were produced by this natural nuclear reaction as are generated in today's reactors. Studies show that the stability of the Gabon geologic formations has allowed these wastes to move less than six feet from where they were formed eons ago.

The search for the sites proved difficult.

Characterizations—defined as a profile of an area's geologic advantages and disadvantages for permanent HLW storage—had to be made of all potential locations. Questions such as the following needed to be answered:

- Are the underground formations solid enough to seal in any radiation leakage from the stored waste?

- Are they stable or will they move too much and threaten to damage the tunnels and the stored casks?

- Are they susceptible to such natural disasters as earthquakes or floods?

- Is there water nearby that will leak into the tunnels and cause them to collapse or corrode the waste canisters and permit radiation to escape?

- Will the location of the repository reduce or increase problems of safely transporting the wastes? How will it affect the costs of transportation?

- Will the site be too close to populated areas?

As if the characterizations were not difficult enough to make, they were joined by another headache. Several states objected to having the installation placed within their borders. Together, the two problems caused the department to announce that work on the search was so complex and moving forward so slowly that it would be impossible to have a repository built and ready to accept waste by the 1998 date specified in the Nuclear Waste Policy Act. The DOE set the opening back to the year 2002 at the earliest. Later, the date was again set back, to 2006. Next, the department said that it was postponing indefinitely the search for the site in the eastern half of the nation and was concentrating its efforts on locales in the West.

The quest now centered on three western locations. Then, in 1987, Congress enacted a new law—the Nuclear Waste Policy Amendments Act.[6] This measure added to the DOE's work—and narrowed the search in the west to just one location.

THE NEW ACT

The Amendments Act added to the DOE's work in two ways. First, it specified that the department was to be responsible for the quality of the casks in which the wastes were shipped to the repository. The department was to make certain that the HLWs were always transported in casks that were certified by the Nuclear Regulatory Commission. To be certified, the casks had to meet certain standards as to their strength and resistance to leakage and breakage by accident. (In DOE terminology, *casks* differ from *canisters*. Casks are the containers in which the wastes will be shipped to their final destination. Canisters are the containers in which they will be actually buried.)

Second, the act ordered the DOE to pick a site for, and then build and operate, what was to be called a Monitored Retrievable Storage (MRS) facility (see Figure 4). An MRS unit is a sort of "halfway house" through which the wastes will pass on their way to final burial. For reasons that will be explained in a later chapter, the wastes will be placed in one type of cask for the first leg of their journey. On reaching the MRS facility, they will be repackaged in other containers and held until they can be sent on to the repository.

Initially, just one MRS unit was planned to serve the entire country. Depending on the rate at which the nation's use of nuclear energy grows over the next years, additional units may soon be needed.

How did the Amendments Act narrow the search for a repository site? Prior to the passage of the measure, the DOE had been studying three principal western locales.[7] They were: Deaf Smith County, Texas; Hanford, Washington; and Yucca Mountain, Nevada. In the new act, Congress told the DOE to forget Deaf Smith County and Hanford. The department was now to focus its site studies solely on Nevada's Yucca Mountain.

Congress saw the other two sites as unworkable for a variety of reasons. There were widespread political and public objections in Texas to the Deaf Smith County site. For one, it lay in the midst of rich and valuable farmland. For another, the construction of the repository tunnels would require that holes be drilled down through two major pools of underground water, one of which is the Ogallala aquifer, a chief water source for the nation's Midwest.

In Washington, the Hanford site had long been favored by the DOE because it is located on the grounds of the Hanford nuclear operation and already has tunnels underground for temporary waste storage. But the site was finally rejected because it is near the Columbia River. Many local residents feared that radiation leakage might contaminate its water. Also, despite the fact that there are tunnels already on the grounds, the construction and operation of a repository there promised to be too costly—some $4 billion more than required for facilities placed at other sites.

The DOE now set its sights on Nevada's Yucca Mountain, a six-mile-long ridge rising above barren desert land near the state's southwestern border. The mountain and the land around it are owned by the federal government. All repository studies were now to be centered here.

In all, the Nuclear Waste Policy Act and the subsequent Amendments Act gave the United States a three-part program for the permanent storage of its commercial and government high-level wastes:

- The establishment and operation of a system for burying the wastes in deep underground tunnels that will be sealed off for thousands of years when filled to capacity.

- The development of a transportation system to carry the wastes safely from the nuclear plants to the burial area.

- The construction of a Monitored Retrievable Storage unit to serve as a "halfway house" for the wastes as they are being moved from the nuclear plants to the repository.

The next chapters will allow us to explore each of these three parts in turn.

7

THE PLACE CALLED YUCCA MOUNTAIN

Along its six-mile length, Yucca Mountain rises 1,000 to 1,500 feet above the surrounding desert land.[1] At one point, it thrusts itself to a summit of 5,575 feet. If you stand there, you can see off to one side Jackass Flats, where the federal government has exploded some 700 nuclear test bombs over the past thirty-eight years. To your other side lies the Nellis Air Force Base Bombing and Gunnery Range, a training area for aerial bombardment. Some 110 miles south and east of your position is the city of Las Vegas. Thirty-eight miles to the west, the Nevada and California borders meet. Just over the California line is Death Valley.

The land stretching away in all directions far below you is wild and desolate, splashed with brush and tufts of tan grass. Earthquake faults run through the area. The cones of several long-dormant volcanoes can be seen in the distance. Yucca Mountain itself was formed by violent volcanic action millions of years ago. The ground directly under your feet is made up of basalt, a darkish igneous rock. Below the surface and thrusting

Yucca Mountain in southwest Nevada is the front-runner choice for the nation's first geologic repository. Information about the mountain's geological and hydrological formations is obtained from exploratory holes drilled around the mountain.

far downward are layers of tuff, rock formations that started as smoking volcanic ash.

Into this mountain, if studies determine it suitable for the job, the DOE intends to drill a honeycomb of tunnels that will permanently hold the nation's commercial and government nuclear high-level wastes. See Figure 5 for a schematic drawing of the mountain.

THE REPOSITORY PLANS

Current plans call for the tunnels to be cut at a depth of 1,000 feet and to total more than 112 miles in length.[2] Spreading out over 1,500 acres, they will be reached by two ramps. The first, inclining downward at a 6-degree angle, will be used to transport the wastes to their final burial place. The second will serve as the "roadway" along which the rock excavated for the tunnels will be brought to the surface.

There will also be four shafts connecting the surface and the repository. They will act as air intakes for workers far underground and will carry equipment and workers to and from the surface.

On the surface—spreading over 150 to 400 acres— will be a waste-handling plant (for receiving and preparing the HLWs for final burial), loading and unloading docks, warehouses, administration buildings, sewage treatment plants, and a security office.

When completed, the repository will be able to house some 63,500 tons of high-level waste, all of it contained in sealed canisters. Most of the waste—approximately 82 percent of the total—will be in solid form and will consist mainly of spent fuel assemblies from the nation's reactors. About 17 percent will be in liquid form and will come from the reprocessing of

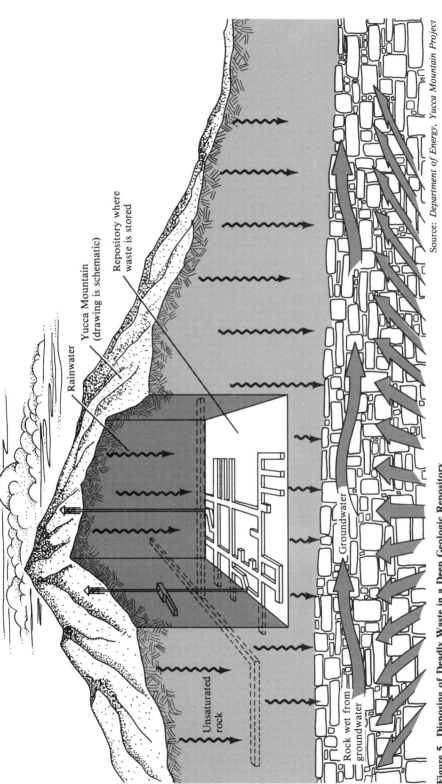

Figure 5. Disposing of Deadly Waste in a Deep Geologic Repository
U.S. Officials believe that the safest method of storing radioactive waste is burial in a deep geologic repository—preferably somewhere dry, stable, and isolated. The DOE is currently evaluating the suitability of Yucca Mountain in the Nevada Desert near Death Valley as a possible site.

Source: *Department of Energy, Yucca Mountain Project*

Rainwater

Yucca Mountain
(drawing is schematic)

Repository where
waste is stored

Unsaturated
rock

Groundwater

Rock wet from
groundwater

spent fuels for defense purposes.* Some low-level waste may also be assigned to the installation.

Rough estimates hold that it may take from twenty-four to twenty-eight years to fill the repository to capacity. Only time—and the rate at which the nation's use of nuclear power grows—will show whether these estimates are accurate.

If the DOE's plans go according to schedule, the studies of Yucca Mountain's suitability would be finished by 1995.[3] Should the site prove satisfactory and be approved for use by Congress, the Nuclear Regulatory Commission would issue a construction license in 1998, with construction itself to begin that same year. The installation would then be built in two phases. The first phase, planned for completion in 2003, would accept wastes for storage during work on the second phase. The entire facility would be operating by 2006. However, in late 1989, the DOE announced that serious delays experienced in the planning stage made it impossible for the repository to be constructed and in operation by the target date given above. According to the DOE, completion may not come until four or more years later.

Finally, once the repository opens, the DOE is to watch how quickly it fills with waste. The department is then to report to Congress as to whether the

---

* In a project having no connection with the Nuclear Waste Policy and Amendments Acts, the federal government has built a repository for the storage of most of the liquid wastes generated in the reprocessing of spent fuels for defense purposes. Located in New Mexico and situated more than 2,000 feet underground, the facility is being plagued by salty water leaking into its tunnels. This water is highly corrosive and can eat through the waste canisters, causing the release of radioactive materials. The presence of the water has caused the DOE to plan on loading the repository to just 2 to 3 percent of its capacity of about 1 million canisters. Each canister contains 55 gallons of waste.

installation is filling so swiftly that it needs to be enlarged or whether an additional facility should be planned and built at another site.

COMPLAINTS AND SUPPORT

Although the Yucca Mountain region is wild and desolate, many Nevadans oppose the idea of having it house a nuclear waste repository.[4] Citing the ever-present possibility of radiation leakage, they consider the repository itself as dangerous. And, citing the presence of nearby earthquake faults and volcanoes (even though the latter are long dormant), they believe the area geologically too dangerous for the safe storage of the wastes. They fear its proximity to an Air Force bombing and gunnery range. And they wonder if it will damage the state's tourist business, especially that of the gambling casinos in Las Vegas.

Accompanying their worry is anger over the congressional decision to limit all site studies to Yucca Mountain and turn their state into what they call "the country's nuclear garbage can." They suspect that the congressional representatives of other states joined in a conspiracy against Nevada and used the decision to get the proposed repository and its dangers out of their own backyards. The feeling is that the states were able to push the decision through because Nevada, with one of the smallest of the nation's congressional delegations, had not sufficient power to fend it off.

Topping off their fears and anger is the suspicion that, with Yucca Mountain now being the only site under investigation, the DOE's studies of it will be biased toward finding it acceptable for the repository, regardless of whether it actually is or not.

In mid-1989, the Nevada Legislature passed a bill

declaring the repository project unlawful. The purpose of the measure was to send a strong warning to the federal government that the state intends to fight the placement of the repository at Yucca Mountain. In December of that year, Nevada filed a legal suit against the federal government in an effort to prevent construction of the repository.

The very idea that the DOE's search is being restricted to just one site—no matter its location—is troubling to some political leaders and scientists both inside and outside Nevada. They feel it unwise, as they put it, to place all the nation's "nuclear eggs in one basket." They argue that, should Yucca Mountain be declared unsuitable for the repository, the United States will be left without a nuclear high-waste disposal program of any sort. The federal government will literally have to start all over again in its quest for a workable site.

Though the Nevada objections to placing the repository at Yucca Mountain are widespread, they are not universally heard in the state. Many Nevadans feel that its remote location makes it ideal for use if its geologic formations do finally prove appropriate for nuclear storage. Many also point out that the construction and operation of the repository will bring increased employment to the state.

On top of all else, the Amendments Act contains a provision that will enrich Nevada with federal monies. The state is to receive $10 million a year while Yucca Mountain is being studied and the repository constructed. Then, throughout the working lifetime of the installation, Nevada will receive annual federal payments of $20 million. If, as estimated, the repository serves for twenty-four to twenty-eight years before being filled to capacity, the total federal payments could amount to well over $600 million.

THE YUCCA MOUNTAIN STUDIES

The big question at the moment, of course, is: Will Yucca Mountain prove to be satisfactory for the repository? We will learn the answer when the characterization studies that are now under way at the mountain are completed.[5] As previously mentioned, a characterization is a profile of the geologic advantages and disadvantages of the site. A wide variety of studies are being conducted by some 1,400 scientists and technicians working in four laboratories sprinkled throughout the area. Here is a look at some of the principal work being done.

Host-Rock Studies
The host-rock is the rock into which the repository tunnels will be carved. Its name is derived from the fact that it will serve as the "host" for the waste canisters. The study of this rock is carried out by examining surface features and drilling exploratory shafts into the below-surface strata.

Much of the host-rock testing is being conducted at Rainier Mesa, a region adjacent to Yucca Mountain. The work here is done in a "laboratory" 1,400 feet underground and located at the end of a mile-long tunnel. Were you to visit the laboratory, you would travel there aboard a roofless metal train that clangs and screeches along tracks running between timbered walls. The darkness is broken now and again by incandescent lights. And, now and again, there are closed passages running off to either side. Signs warn that these passages are stained with radioactive contamination. A quarter of a century ago, they were used for underground tests of nuclear weapons.

The tunnel at last widens into a large room. Here, workers drill out samples of the rock and then put them through various stress and pressure tests. The object is to determine if the host-rock is stable and strong enough to remain in place and resist shifts in the earth over the next 10,000 years and, at the same time, handle a complex of other problems.

High on the list of those other problems are such questions as: Is the rock tough enough to keep from melting and destroying the tunnels when enduring the tremendous heat emitted by the wastes? Is it solid enough to help protect the canisters against corrosive water seepage from the surrounding strata? Water is a double villain here; not only can it corrode the canisters and cause them to leak radioactive materials but it can also carry those materials into the surrounding strata. Then there is the question of whether the rock is solid enough to slow or prevent the advance of radiation into the strata or the outer environment.

Exactly what kind of stress and pressure testing is the rock undergoing at Rainier Mesa? One experiment centers on the intense heat that would flow from the wastes. To see how well the rock can endure this heat without melting into a molten mass that will destroy the canisters, workers first cut an eight-foot-square block out of a laboratory wall and then drill holes into its top and sides. Next they place heaters, representing the hot waste, into the holes, after which pressure is exerted on the block by steel devices. Various instruments measure the temperature and pressure to which the rock is being subjected and gauge how successfully it is standing up to both.

In another test, pressure is applied to the block

from various angles. Simultaneously, the block is heated to a temperature of 212 degrees Fahrenheit to drive out whatever amount of water it contains. Once deprived of its water content, the block is pumped full of new water. The purpose here is to test the strength of the host-rock by exposing it to a wide variety of tortures.

The workers at Rainier Mesa seem confident that the host-rock will prove suitable for the wastes. It is made up of tuff, a type of rock that began as burning ash when the area was hit by violent volcanic action between 13 and 18 million years ago. It is a rock that can be porous or nonporous or a combination of the two. Beneath Yucca Mountain, it divides itself into four major layers that extend to a depth of 6,500 feet. The DOE plans to situate the repository in a layer made up chiefly of the nonporous type, which is called densely welded tuff.

Following that long-ago volcanic action, the densely welded tuff cooled and solidified more slowly than the porous type (known as nonwelded tuff). Consequently, it is less crumbly and far stronger than the nonwelded variety. It is so strong, in fact, that it has a compressive strength twelve times that of concrete and will give construction crews trouble when they try to drill through it. Thus, though it contains some porous areas and though it is marked with many cracks and crevices, it promises to do well against heat, the invasion of corrosive water, and shifts in the earth for the next 10,000 years.

It is especially vital that the rock be solid enough to lock in any radiation leaking from a corroded canister. The canisters are expected to resist the effects of corrosion for a period of up to 1,000 years. After that length of time, leakage is to be expected. The rock will have the job of keeping the radiation in place and slowing or preventing its escape into the environment.

The densely welded tuff is expected to do particularly well in one respect. It is known as a good conductor of heat. This will enable the rock to absorb and pass on the heat from the wastes without melting and becoming a dangerous and destructive molten mass. In addition, suppose that underground water seeps into its cracks and crevices. Its fractured structure will allow steam to escape toward the surface and dissipate if the water, heated by the wastes, ever reaches the boiling point. The waste canisters would be protected from the steam's corrosive effect.*

Water Studies

With Death Valley, the driest area in North America, lying just thirty-eight miles away, the Yucca Mountain region is, not surprisingly, hot and arid. It receives an average of just three to six inches of rain annually. Yet, despite this scant rainfall, the DOE studies are focusing much of their attention on the dangers of water to the repository.

Though the densely welded tuff promises to help protect the tunnels against water seeping in from the surrounding earth, these studies are considered of vital

---

* Until recently, scientific theory held that salt formations would serve best for a repository, in great part because it was thought that their ability to seal fissures in their structure would efficiently lock in any leaking radiation. The federal repository for reprocessed HLWs in New Mexico was carved into a salt formation, and the leakage problems it is suffering have cast serious doubt on this theory. The welded tuff at Yucca Mountain is now widely considered superior to salt as a "host" for the wastes.

*Sample soils taken from Yucca Mountain are tested
for their ability to store radioactive wastes. The site
is rich in tuff, a type of rock made up of solidified
volcanic ash ideal for nuclear waste containment.*

importance because of the possibility of flash floods and future changes in the area's climate. Should something happen that allows water to come through the host-rock and corrode the waste canisters, it would release a radiation that could then work its way up to the surface or down to an aquifer that lies 2,000 feet below the mountain. An aquifer is an underground source of water embedded in porous rock. The aquifer would likewise be threatened if liquid wastes escaped from their canisters and oozed down toward it.

It is to help reduce the dangers of radiation leakage that the repository is planned for a depth of 1,000 feet —a depth that is exactly halfway between the surface and the aquifer. The area at this level is called an unsaturated zone. Above it are strata containing rainwater that has been absorbed into the earth; below are strata permeated with water from the aquifer. But the unsaturated zone itself is without any appreciable amount of water. It is below the reach of the water near the surface, and above the reach of the water in the aquifer. Of the three western sites that were originally considered for the repository, only Yucca Mountain boasts an unsaturated zone.

Scientists at Yucca Mountain say that the lack of water in the unsaturated zone promises much for the safety of the wastes. But the absence of water is not the only advantage offered. Because the average rainfall is only three to six inches a year and because much of its moisture is evaporated by the area's heat, only a scant amount of water ever manages to penetrate the earth in the first place. The scientists estimate that, of that small amount, only 0.02 inches of the annual rainfall will ever work its way down to the 1,000-foot-deep repository. It will not be enough to do any harm.

But suppose that, for some reason, the waste canisters do corrode or break open? The scientists claim that the aquifer will be well protected. Should either solid or liquid waste escape, each would take about 10,000 years to inch down to the level of the aquifer. By that time, the radioactivity will have lost its power to poison the valuable water.

Though there is little rainfall at Yucca Mountain now, what does the future hold for the region? There have been major climatic changes in various parts of the world over the centuries (for example, vast sections of the earth were once covered by masses of ice) and there is no reason to believe that Yucca Mountain's climate will not change at some point in the future, perhaps bringing heavy annual rainfall that would soak through to the repository. Consequently, much of the Yucca Mountain study is devoted to gauging what the climate there might be like 1,000 or 10,000 years from now.

One major study is exploring clues to the future by investigating the surrounding life in the past. Being researched are the fossilized remains of animals, among them pack rats. By looking at the materials that went into their nests—twigs, leaves, and such—an idea can be formed as to whether the region was once wet or always dry.

Troubling the DOE workers is a water theory held by a physical scientist named Jerry Szymanski. He believes the Yucca Mountain region is currently in the midst of a geologic disruption that causes the underground rock formations to contract and expand. Szymanski bases his theory on the current levels of stress that have been noted in the formations. He says that these disruptive cycles occur every 20,000 to 30,000 years and that they are capable of causing the area's aquifer to shift its position upward by 1,000 feet. If his theory is correct, the aquifer could rise at some point in the future and flood the repository—perhaps with devastating results.

DOE representatives say that Szymanski's theory is being closely investigated in the characterization studies at the mountain. If the theory does prove to be true, it could, in the minds of some scientists, put an end to the planned repository.

Volcanic Studies
Yucca Mountain is circled by the cones of dormant volcanoes. The DOE study of these volcanoes is aimed at determining the odds of their erupting again one day. One investigation is concentrating on the cone known as Lathrop Wells Volcano, which stands about twelve miles away. The researchers have found indications that it might be a mere 5,000 years old. In the opinion of some of the scientists, the relative youth of the volcano increases the chance that it will someday erupt again.

Other researchers are not worried about the possibility of damaging eruptions at Lathrop Wells or elsewhere. They contend that, while Yucca Mountain itself was born of violent volcanic action, the volcanoes around it were formed in a gentler manner—by eruptions that caused lava to ooze from their tops and not by explosions that sent rock and burning ash spewing out for miles around. If this is true, then the Lathrop Wells Volcano and its surrounding cones would likely not damage the repository should they again act up. Experiments are now being conducted to assess the manner in which the volcanoes actually came into being.

Among those not deeply worried about future volcanic action is Robert Raup, the coordinator of the

U.S. Geologic Survey in Denver, Colorado. Raup believes that the chances of an eruption right at the repository site are not great. He bases his opinion on what has been seen of shifts in the earth's crust at Yucca Mountain. The shifts do not, in his opinion, suggest the danger of volcanic explosions.

Earthquake Studies

Since Yucca Mountain lies among earthquake faults, many Nevadans are worried by the possibility of future tremors and the dangers they might pose for the repository. Over the past 130 years or so, eight major earthquakes (measuring 6.5 or more on the Richter Scale) have struck within 250 miles of Yucca Mountain. Seismologists at the site are not unduly concerned by the fact that Yucca Mountain is bound to be shaken from time to time and are wondering whether any earthquake research will be necessary. They believe that the repository will not be significantly affected because it will lie 1,000 feet underground. The force of an earthquake diminishes considerably as it descends to that depth.

They do believe, however, that earthquakes will be a problem for the repository's surface facilities. Since nuclear waste will be given its final preparations at the surface, it is there that the greatest danger lurks. Seismologists will play a major role in deciding on the safest locations for the surface facilities and in advising on the types of structure most resistant to quake damage.

Though the repository itself is expected to be filled in a period of twenty-four to twenty-eight years, the surface facilities will remain in use for years afterward, checking on the wastes and watching for any problems that might occur underground.

8

THE ROAD
TO BURIAL

Once the repository is built at Yucca Mountain—or
elsewhere if such proves to be necessary—the government and a number of commercial companies will face
the job of safely moving the wastes to it. This task
brings us to the second and third parts of the nation's
waste disposal program: the development of a transportation system and the construction of a Monitored
Retrievable Storage (MRS) unit to serve as a "halfway
house" for the wastes while they are en route to the
repository. Figure 6 explains the different functions of
an integrated MRS facility.

WORKING TOGETHER

The transportation system and the MRS unit will work
together. Current DOE plans call for them to handle
the wastes as follows.[1]

First, the wastes will be packaged in casks at the
power plants and then moved to the MRS unit by
truck or rail—or by barge if there are nearby rivers

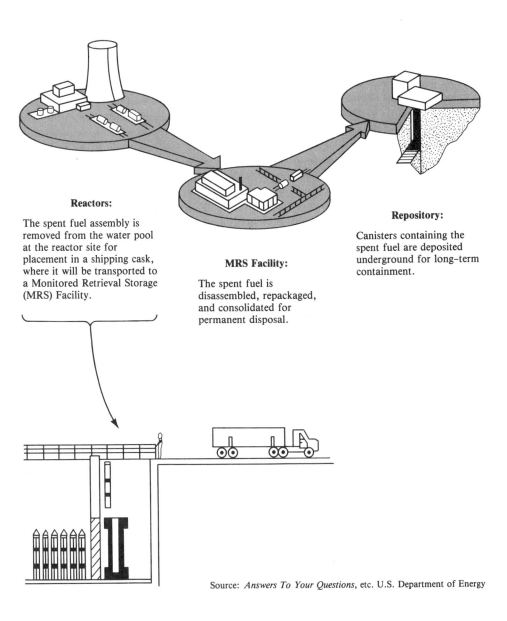

Reactors:

The spent fuel assembly is removed from the water pool at the reactor site for placement in a shipping cask, where it will be transported to a Monitored Retrieval Storage (MRS) Facility.

MRS Facility:

The spent fuel is disassembled, repackaged, and consolidated for permanent disposal.

Repository:

Canisters containing the spent fuel are deposited underground for long-term containment.

Source: *Answers To Your Questions*, etc. U.S. Department of Energy

Figure 6. Nuclear Waste Distribution and Disposal in a System with an MRS Facility

along which they can be more conveniently sent. Next, for reasons we shall see in a moment, the MRS workers will remove the wastes from the casks and repackage them in canisters, which will then be placed in other casks for the remainder of the journey to the repository. You may recall that the DOE defines casks as the containers in which the wastes will travel, while canisters are the containers in which they will be buried.

Finally, the run from the MRS unit to the repository is presently planned to be made by rail. Upon arrival at the repository, the wastes will go to a surface-level receiving-and-handling station to be readied for burial.

At present, only one MRS unit is planned for the nation, but more may be needed in the future as the use of nuclear power grows. So that most journeys to the unit will be relatively short ones and thus reduce the chances of highway or other accidents, the DOE intends to place the facility in a spot as close as possible to the greatest number of power plants. Accordingly, the department plans to situate it in the central-eastern area of the country, where most of today's commercial nuclear plants are clustered. The DOE also anticipates that some shipments, especially those from plants far in the West, may skip the MRS unit and move directly to the repository.

Why the MRS Unit?
But now two questions: If some shipments will go straight to the repository, why is the MRS unit necessary? Why can't all the shipments make their way directly to final burial?[2]

The answer lies in the fact that some 82 percent of

the wastes will be in solid form, with most being spent fuel assemblies. Fuel assemblies, you'll remember, are made up of the stainless steel or zirconium rods into which uranium pellets are inserted for fissioning. The rods measure from three to fourteen feet in length and are about a half-inch in diameter. They are bundled together in assemblies of between 30 and 300 each for insertion into a reactor. The assemblies must be replaced (usually every two to three years) when they become so shot through with radioactivity that they are no longer able to perform efficiently during the fissioning process. It is then that they are listed as spent fuel assemblies.

Strapped together in bundles of 30 to 300 rods, the assemblies are bulky and clumsy things. At the MRS unit they can be taken apart to reduce their overall bulk and make it possible to incorporate the dismantled connective gear and rods from several casks into one larger container. Fewer casks will then have to travel on to the repository. The aim is to have less waste on the move during the final run to the repository—a run that will be longer than most trips from the power plants to the MRS unit.

But why not take the assemblies apart and place them in the larger casks right at the start of the journey? The answer is that this job requires its own personnel, a special building, and special equipment. The expense involved would be astronomical if every one of the country's nuclear plants were to do its own dismantling. It is far more economical to place the necessary building, equipment, and manpower in a single, conveniently situated MRS unit—or a series of units if necessary.

Along with saving money and reducing the number of trips to the repository, the MRS unit will offer a third advantage. It will be able to keep the wastes in storage until the times when the repository is best able to handle them.

TRANSPORTING THE WASTES

Three government agencies share the major responsibility for the transportation system.[3] They are: the DOE's Office of Civilian Radioactive Waste Management (OCRWM), the U.S. Department of Transportation (DOT), and the Nuclear Regulatory Commission (NRC).

The OCRWM holds the overall responsibility for the shipment of the wastes. The Department of Transportation is charged with several responsibilities. It must set up regulations governing the loading, unloading, and handling of the wastes. It must also see that the waste casks are properly labeled and that the trucks, railroad cars, and barges carrying them are marked with signs warning the public of the hazardous materials on board.

In addition, it must see that all personnel involved in the system are trained in the handling of the wastes. Special attention is to be given to all truck drivers. They must not only be trained but also certified for their work. Finally, the Department must check the routes that will be traveled and certify that they can be safely used.

The Nuclear Regulatory Commission likewise holds several responsibilities. It must develop procedures to safeguard the traveling wastes from theft and sabotage. And it must notify the states and Indian tribes of shipments that will be passing through their lands. One of its most interesting jobs is that of overseeing the design and performance of the casks to be used in shipment and making certain that they are strong and durable enough for their work.

The Shipping Casks

A number of casks of different sizes have already been developed for use.[4] Some are meant to be carried aboard trucks to the MRS unit; they weigh between 25 and 40 tons and are built to hold from one to seven spent fuel assemblies. Larger models—weighing up to 200 tons and intended for the railroad cars that will travel on to the repository—can accommodate thirty-six or more assemblies. Regardless of size and weight, the casks are tubular in shape. They can range up to 12 feet in diameter and 22 feet in length.

The wall of a typical cask is six to eight inches thick and is divided into three parts. There is an outer hide of stainless steel and an inner shell, also of stainless steel. Between the two is a layer of shielding material, customarily lead, to lock in the cargo's radioactivity. All casks must be designed so that they can survive the most severe road, rail, and water accidents without splitting or breaking open and releasing hazardous radioactivity.

The job of designing and manufacturing the casks has been given to private industry. Whenever a new type of cask is designed and developed, it is required to meet certain endurance standards, set by the NRC, before it can be cleared for use. To meet these standards, the new cask must undergo a series of tests to check its design, materials, and construction for their ability to survive mechanical, fire, and water mishaps.

Here are several "torture" tests developed by the National Academy of Sciences that the casks endured:

In one test, a cask was dropped from a helicopter. It hit the desert ground at 235 miles per hour and dug

itself four feet into the hard-packed soil. The only damage suffered was some scratched paint.

In a test to check resistance to punctures, a cask was dropped more than three feet onto the upthrust end of a steel bar that was 6 inches in diameter and 8 inches long. The cask was dented but suffered no splits or punctures.

To see how it would behave in a fiery crash, a cask was strapped aboard a railroad car and sent crashing into a thick concrete wall at 81 miles an hour. Both car and cask were then engulfed in a jet fuel fire that lasted 125 minutes. The fire caused the lead shield between the cask's inner and outer walls to melt. After about 100 minutes of intense burning, a small crack about as thick as the edge of a dollar bill appeared in the cask's outer skin and some molten lead from the shield oozed out. However, the simulated radioactive materials deep inside the cask remained where they were.

The damage led to the cask being redesigned. In a repeat of the test, the shielding capacity in the new design prevented most of the molten lead from escaping. Again, the simulated radioactive materials inside the cask remained in place.

An even more spectacular test was conducted in Great Britain in 1984. A cask was placed on the flatbed of a truck that was then rammed by a diesel locomotive. The locomotive was pulling three 35-ton cars and moving at 100 miles an hour at the moment of impact.

This shipping cask is designed to remove used fuel assemblies from nuclear reactors and transport them for burial.

The entire train was totally destroyed. The cask—after being hurled 200 feet along the tracks—sustained only minor scratches.

To test for water-tightness, a cask was submerged in 3 feet of water and left there for 8 hours. It was then lowered to a depth of 50 feet and left there for another 8 hours.

The new cask undergoes the accident, fire, and water tests in sequence to determine their cumulative effects on its design, materials, and construction. When it has survived all three tests it will be certified for use by the NRC and its mass production can begin. The certification lasts for five years, with inspections along the way to make sure that the container is performing as expected.

Actually, though the United States is only now preparing to build its first permanent HLW repository and making plans for the transport of the wastes to it, work on the casks has been going on for some time. Anticipating the time when there would be a permanent storage place, the government asked the National Academy of Sciences to develop the cask tests in the 1970s. The Transportation Technology Center at the Sandia National Laboratories conducted its first tests in the mid-1970s.

The shipping of nuclear materials is also not new in the United States. The country has been transporting such materials by road, rail, and inland water for more than forty years. The shipments, varying in size from small packages upward, have involved low-level wastes from work done in medicine, industry, power production, and research. And many have carried the wastes to the commercial and federal dumps mentioned in Chapter Three. The Department of Energy claims that these shipments have not caused a single death or injury from escaping radioactivity.

The Methods of Transportation

Truck, train, and barge are the three transportation vehicles planned for use in the shipment of the HLWs.[5] When carried by rail from the MRS unit to the repository, the wastes will be placed aboard dedicated trains, meaning trains that will be used only for the transport of nuclear materials. Railroad cars carrying HLWs are not to be attached to trains hauling general freight.

The Nuclear Waste Policy Act specifies that the DOE contract with private industry in developing and operating the transportation system. While private industry will do the actual shipping, it will work under guidelines and regulations maintained by the DOE, the NRC, and the Department of Transportation. To see how the system will work, imagine that you are a truck driver assigned the job of moving a load of waste from a power plant to the Monitored Retrievable Storage unit.

Before your trip begins, empty shipping casks are delivered to the power plant.[6] They are unloaded and moved to the water tanks where the spent fuel assemblies have been temporarily stored. The assemblies are removed by plant workers using special hoists (sometimes called master-slave devices) and deposited in the shipping cask that your truck will carry.

The cask is checked for radioactive contamination. Checklists are reviewed to make sure that the cask meets federal regulations—regulations that govern such matters as the levels of heat on its surface. Once cleared for travel, the cask is swung aboard your truck and locked in place behind a metal barrier to prevent anyone from accidentally or deliberately reaching the container and trying to open or damage it. The cask is labeled to show the type of cargo it is carrying. Placards warning the public that your truck is carrying hazardous materials are placed on the cab and trailer. You are handed a certificate saying that the cask meets all federal and state regulations for shipment. A final inspection of the truck, trailer, and cargo is made by federal and state officials and you are at last ready to pull out.

Since your rig meets all the federal and state vehicle requirements, you are free to travel on the same interstate and state highways and bridges used by other motorists. However, the Department of Transportation urges that you take bypasses and beltways around cities and towns whenever possible. Also, the states through which you'll travel may require that you use selected alternate routes. If so, they must fall within the DOT's guidelines for safe use.

Throughout your trip, you must carry a written plan of your route to the MRS unit. This plan includes your point of origin and your destination, estimated times of departure and arrival, planned stops, and telephone numbers for emergency assistance in each state through which you will pass. You are under orders not

Technicians at a nuclear plant in Buchanan, New York, supervise the loading of low-level radioactive waste for shipment to a dumping site.

to leave your truck and its dangerous cargo unattended and to make stops only for food, fuel, rest, needed vehicle repairs, and the mandatory state, NRC, and Department of Transportation inspections that will be made along the way.

Despite all the regulations and safety requirements —and despite all the training you received before being permitted to handle a nuclear shipment—there is always the possibility of a roadway accident. Should there be an accident, you are to assist the fire and police personnel who arrive at the scene. With them, you are to follow specific guidelines established by the DOE's Federal Emergency Management Agency. These guidelines include the following procedures:

• Administer lifesaving measures to anyone injured in the accident.

• Ascertain whether any radioactive materials have been released and review the information that you carry on the hazardous materials.

• Contact the proper authorities to obtain advice on how to deal with any escaping materials and their dangers.

• Determine and carry out whatever actions are necessary to prevent further harm to life or property.

On the third point, the United States maintains eight emergency-response regions with experts available to respond with assistance in case of accident. These regions have their headquarters at: Upton, New York; Oak Ridge, Tennessee; Aiken, South Carolina; Argonne, Illinois; Albuquerque, New Mexico; Idaho

Falls, Idaho; Oakland, California; and Richland, Washington. Any of these offices can assemble an emergency-response team within two hours and have it on the scene of an accident within eight hours. You will carry the list of their telephone numbers throughout your trip.

In the event your truck is attacked by terrorists intent on stealing your cargo, your call for help will be handled by the DOE's Nuclear Emergency Search Team and a DOE Radiological Assistance Team. Both are specially trained to handle cases of attack, theft, and sabotage. There are twenty-eight DOE Radiological Assistance Teams made up of federal and contract personnel available to give you assistance.

To help you further, the DOE—through its Radioactive Materials Hazard Awareness Workshops—offers special training to state and local police, fire department personnel, and emergency response teams. The Department of Transportation also publishes training materials and offers slide programs to the states for use by their police, fire, and emergency personnel.

But let's say that your truck makes its way without incident to the Monitored Retrievable Storage unit. What will you find there?

THE MONITORED RETRIEVABLE STORAGE UNIT

As currently planned, the MRS unit will have three basic facilities in addition to such features as administrative and security offices.[7] At the receiving-and-handling building the wastes will be unloaded and then repackaged for the next step in their journey.

The monitored-storage building will house any wastes that must be held at the MRS unit until the

This truck is used to transport radioactive waste from the nuclear power plants to temporary storage facilities.

time when they can best be sent on to the repository. The term *monitored* means that the wastes will be steadily watched for signs of radiation leakage and other problems. The concrete casks in which the wastes will be kept while in temporary storage at the unit will be produced in the concrete-manufacturing building.

On arriving in the receiving-and-handling building, the spent fuel assemblies will be dismantled to separate the fuel rods from the hardware that holds them together. The rods will then be rearranged in tighter formations. The remaining parts—the gear that once held them in bundles—will be compressed. The rods and gear will then be placed in steel canisters, after which the canisters will either be placed in temporary storage or locked in large railroad casks for an immediate run to the repository.

Much of the work in the receiving-and-handling building will be done by personnel working behind heavy shields to protect them from exposure to radiation. As an added precaution, the waste material will be manipulated by remote control.

Both the Nuclear Waste Policy Act and Amendments Act specify that the decision on where to locate the MRS unit is not to be made until after a site for the repository itself is selected. The MRS decision is being held in abeyance until the Yucca Mountain studies are completed and the Nevada site, if found suitable, is approved for use by Congress. At present, as you know, the DOE hopes to locate the MRS unit somewhere in the central-eastern region of the country because it is there that most of the nation's commercial nuclear power plants are to be found.

When the DOE does begin its MRS search, all sites that come under consideration will be submitted to characterization studies similar to those being carried out at Yucca Mountain. Each site will have its geological traits evaluated. Practical aspects to be considered include proximity to necessary transportation facilities (highways, railroads, rivers, and rights of way), the availability of public utilities, and the extra expenses of construction that the site's location and terrain might entail.

Additionally, the studies will attempt to gauge the effects that the MRS unit will have on the local environment and surrounding communities. The hope here is to place the unit where it will have the least number of unfavorable consequences for the people living nearby. This particular investigation will be done by examining the area's existing environmental, social, and economic conditions and ascertaining how they will be changed—positively, negatively, or not at all— by the presence of the unit.

The current schedule for locating and building the facility calls for the DOE to select all potential sites by 1992 and to make a final choice by 1993. As holds true for the repository, a construction license must then be obtained from the NRC; the DOE's application for that license is slated for 1995, with the license (if all goes without a hitch) expected to be issued by 1997. Construction of the unit is anticipated to begin in 1998, with the unit to be open and operating by 2003.

FINAL BURIAL

The DOE says that it is committed to careful and safe handling of the wastes both during shipment and while housed at the MRS unit. This insistence on safety can also be seen in the plans for handling the wastes at their final destination.[8] At repository's receiving-and-handling station, the casks will be unloaded and their canisters removed. Then the canisters themselves will be opened and their contents prepared for transfer to other canisters—the ones in which they will finally be buried.

Why must the canisters be opened? Present DOE plans call for the wastes to be fused with a protective material that will help to lock in their radioactive contents more securely. The material to be used is borosilicate glass, an extremely strong substance that can easily be produced on a large scale.

The borosilicate glass will be in molten form when the wastes are mixed with it. (Workers will do the mixing by remote control to safeguard against radioactive contamination.) While still in a molten state, the glass and its wastes will be poured into stainless steel canisters, called pour canisters. Then, when the mixture has cooled and solidified, the pour canisters will be plugged and welded shut. They will be tested for leaks and decontaminated. Decontamination will remove any radioactive residue from their outer sides.

But there is still more to the preparation for burial. The pour canisters will then be inserted into what are known as burial containers. These containers are to serve as partitions between the waste-filled pour canisters and the repository environment. They are to be constructed of carbon steel, stainless steel, or copper-based alloys; each of these metals would resist corrosion if exposed to such geologic conditions as the invasion of water into the repository tunnels. Only when the burial containers have at last been closed and sealed will the wastes be moved into the tunnels for permanent storage.

The DOE believes that all aspects of its planned disposal program—the geology of Yucca Mountain (should the site prove suitable for use), the repository depth of 1,000 feet, the carefully maintained transportation program and MRS unit, the bonding of the wastes with borosilicate glass, and the placement of the pour canisters within burial containers—will provide the nation with maximum protection against the dangers of leaking radioactive materials, not only for the present but for all the 10,000 years needed for the wastes to decay to the point where they are no longer harmful.

And what of that year sometime in the early twenty-first century when the repository reaches its capacity of some 63,500 tons of waste?[9] Its tunnels will be filled with dirt, sealed off, and then constantly monitored for any sign of escaping radiation. The surface area at Yucca Mountain will be decontaminated and allowed to return to its original state.

To protect future generations of tourists and campers from accidentally intruding on the closed repository, the DOE is considering, on the recommendation of the Environmental Protection Agency, a plan to dot the area with warning symbols and messages that can be seen from both the air and the ground. These messages must be unmistakably clear to everyone because they will be seen by people who speak many different languages. Further, languages may change—and some may vanish—in the course of 10,000 years. To ensure their absolute clarity, the messages are now being prepared by the DOE with the help of experts from several fields.

Working on them are anthropologists (whose studies include human culture and environment), epigraphers (who study such phenomena as the markings on ancient buildings and monuments), linguists (who study human speech), archaeologists (who investigate past human life as revealed by fossil relics and artifacts left by ancient people), and psychologists (who study behavior and the mind).

Finally, information on the repository and its location will be placed in public libraries, real estate deed and title offices, computer centers, and time capsules. The information will also be filed with appropriate authorities throughout the world. All this will be done to insure against the possibility of the repository records ever being lost over the span of the next 100 centuries.

9
___

THE WORLD STORY

___

More than twenty-five nations use nuclear power today. They all face the same problems as the United
States when dealing with the disposal of their nuclear
wastes. Let's examine how they handle these problems
in four parts.

PART ONE:
PERMANENT STORAGE OF
HIGH-LEVEL WASTES

The nuclear nations are located in all parts of the
world and vary greatly in size.[1] They range from such
small countries as South Korea and Switzerland to
such giants as Canada and India. All use nuclear energy to generate a percentage of their electrical power.
But that percentage is as varied among the countries as
are their sizes. It ranges from lows of around 3 percent
(in Italy, for example) to highs of over 60 percent (in
France). Overall, nearly half the countries depend on

nuclear power for more than 25 percent of their electrical needs.

In the matter of disposal, most of the nations seem to like the system being developed by the United States for the permanent storage of HLWs—placement in an underground repository, with the wastes locked in borosilicate glass to help protect against leakage of radioactive materials. Here is a rundown of what ten representative nations are planning to do with their high-level wastes, along with notes on the amounts of nuclear power being produced by the countries. (The numbers of reactors listed below are based on statistics gathered in the late 1980s. They are subject to change as the countries open new power plants.)

Belgium
Belgium is served by seven nuclear reactors that produce approximately 60 percent of its electricity. The nation is considering the use of an underground repository for its HLWs. The advisability of building the installation in clay strata is currently being studied. Belgium plans to begin testing the burial of canisters in the clay in the mid-1990s.

Canada
More than 12 percent of Canada's electrical power is generated by fifteen nuclear reactors. Plans for the permanent burial of HLWs are focusing on stable rock formations in the Canadian Shield, a vast plateau that stretches across much of northern, central, and eastern Canada. Specific steps in the plans call for characterization studies of various potential locations, the selection of a site, and then, before the repository itself is built, the construction and operation of a demonstration burial vault to test for possible problems.

Federal Republic Of Germany
(West Germany)

West Germany's nineteen reactors generate more than 30 percent of the country's electricity. At present, West Germany's high-level wastes are stored at a facility near Gorleben in the German state of Lower Saxony. Studies are under way to determine if a nearby salt formation will prove suitable for a permanent underground repository. The studies are scheduled to be completed in the early 1990s.

Finland

Four reactors—two of which were built by the Soviet Union—generate some 40 percent of Finland's electrical power. The nation hopes to send the high-level wastes created by the two Soviet-built reactors to the Soviet Union for permanent burial after keeping them stored at the reactor sites for five years. Though Finland would like to have all its HLWs permanently stored outside its borders, the country is studying the possibility of burying the wastes from its other two reactors in granite bedrock formations somewhere in the Finnish countryside.

France

About 65 percent of French electrical power is generated by more than forty reactors. France intends to build an underground repository for the permanent storage of its HLWs. The installation will likely be

This French nuclear reactor produced plutonium material for an atomic bomb that the French exploded over the Sahara Desert in 1960.

carved into granite, clay, salt, or schist (a metamorphic crystalline type of rock) strata. After a potential repository site is selected, by the early 1990s, a subterranean test laboratory will be built there. The laboratory will be used for experiments to gauge the locale's suitability for permanent storage. If the site is then approved for the repository, France does not expect to be burying its wastes there before the year 2010.

Great Britain

Great Britain's thirty-seven reactors provide the nation with more than 20 percent of its electrical power. At present, British high-level wastes are temporarily stored in various locations: at the commercial reactor sites, at the government's Sellafield reprocessing plant (see Chapter Four), and in several above-ground facilities. The nation once thought about drilling an underground repository into a granite formation in northern Scotland. After various studies were made of the site, however, the project was called off and further plans postponed until international researches into HLW disposal give indications of the permanent storage system best suited for the country.

India

India has six reactors that supply the country with about 2 percent of its electricity. The nation is presently looking at a number of sites that may serve a repository well. India, however, has a problem regarding the transportation of wastes to a permanent burial spot. It lacks a modern highway system and adequate railroads. For the present, the country is planning to store its nuclear wastes at the power plants.

Italy

Three reactors supply 3 percent of Italy's electrical power. Italy plans to bury its HLWs in clay deposits and is now in the midst of a study of possible repository sites. A subterranean test installation in Sicily has been established.

Japan
Over 25 percent of Japan's electrical power comes from the nation's thirty-three nuclear plants. The Japanese are presently researching a number of locations for an underground repository. In the main, they are looking at sites that have granite, tuff, or diabase (a finely grained type of altered basaltic rock) formations. If plans go according to schedule, a trial site for the repository will be chosen by 1995 and the test burials of HLW canisters in tunnels drilled there will commence in 2015.

Sweden
Though its twelve reactors provide Sweden with more than 50 percent of its electricity, the country plans to abandon its use of nuclear power by 2010, the year when the reactors will reach the end of their estimated operating lives. Sweden plans to bury the wastes that have accumulated over the years in a granite underground repository. A number of possible sites for the facility are now being investigated. Selection of a final site is expected by 2000.

PART TWO:
LOW-LEVEL WASTES
AND REPROCESSING

The second part of the world story centers on two different decisions—first, those that have been made concerning the disposal of low-level wastes and those being made for the reprocessing of spent fuel for military purposes.[2]

Three systems are currently used for the disposal

of the low-level wastes that are created in nuclear production, weapons manufacture, medicine, and research. Some nations employ the U.S. system of shallow burial on selected lands. Others, despite the dangers involved, continue to dump their wastes at sea. And still others are using abandoned mines as LLW cemeteries.

Some countries—Canada, France, Great Britain, Italy, and Japan among them—are either currently reprocessing or planning to reprocess spent fuel so that its uranium and plutonium content can be reused. They plan to dispose of the high-level waste resulting from reprocessing by burying it in their underground repositories. The spent fuel, which is itself a high-level waste, will be held at power-plant sites or at reprocessing centers until ready for handling.

Other nations, such as Switzerland and Spain, do not plan to enter into reprocessing. At present, Switzerland intends to ship its spent fuel out of the country for reprocessing. Spain wants to do no reprocessing whatsoever, either inside or outside its borders. The nations that plan to avoid the procedure will eventually consign their spent fuel to their underground repositories.

Several countries—in particular, France and Japan—are willing to accept spent fuel from other nations and reprocess it for them. France, however, has said it will not store the resultant HLWs, but will ship them back to the customer countries. Nor does France intend to store permanently any other wastes generated by outsiders.

PART THREE:
PROBLEMS AND TENSIONS

Some nuclear nations are experiencing trouble with their neighbors.[3] Much of the trouble is centered in

Europe and stems from two roots—fright over the consequences of the Chernobyl disaster and the fact that 119 of Europe's nuclear reactors are located within 30 kilometers of neighboring borders. The neighbors loathe the idea of having what they see as the source of potential catastrophes lying so close to them.

The situation has led to a number of confrontations in recent years. Denmark, for example, has asked Sweden to close a plant situated some 30 kilometers from the Danish border. West Germany has asked France to stop the construction of four nearby plants; the request has been refused. Disputes over the use of nuclear energy and the placement of reactors have erupted between Ireland and Great Britain and, elsewhere, between Argentina and Chile, and Hong Kong and China.

A quite different problem is now causing worldwide anger and concern. Recent reports indicate that nuclear wastes have become a part of a larger disposal problem. For several years now, a number of industrial nations, including the United States, have shipped their industrial wastes elsewhere for disposal. These products are known variously as hazardous or toxic wastes and consist of such "garbage" as chemicals, sludges, fertilizers, and pesticide residue.

For the most part, the shipments have gone to Third World countries in Africa and Latin America— nations desperately in need of the money they can charge for accepting the refuse, but nations that are underdeveloped and without the facilities for its safe and secure disposal.

The practice of exporting toxic garbage—especially to countries ill-prepared to handle it—has angered thoughtful people everywhere. They see it as contaminating the earth and water of the recipient nations and threatening the health and lives of the populations.

The exporting countries are seen as cold-bloodedly dumping their wastes on somebody else to get the stuff out of their own backyards and to save money. The fees charged by the financially desperate recipients are far less than the costs of disposing of the toxics at home.

Worldwide anger over the practice has intensified since news reports from Africa revealed that shipments of hazardous toxics to Nigeria and several surrounding states have included some nuclear wastes. The Africans report that the shipments came from Europe. They have angrily announced that they will no longer accept European hazardous wastes.

At present, it is not known whether the United States is including nuclear materials in its export of hazardous waste. The United States sends some of its hazardous wastes to Africa, the Caribbean area, and South America for disposal. Some are also handled by modern disposal facilities in Canada.

PART FOUR:
INTERNATIONAL COOPERATION

The fourth part of the world story turns from disputes and tensions to international programs of nuclear research.[4] A number of nations are working together toward a better understanding of how to handle nuclear energy and its wastes.

For example, eight nations are presently engaged in a study of granite formations and the way in which water flows through this type of rock. The nations are Canada, Finland, France, Great Britain, Japan, Sweden, Switzerland, and the United States. The study is being conducted at a mine site in central Sweden.

Another example: Since 1981, West Germany and the United States have been working together on a number of tests in a German subterranean laboratory. The aim of the tests is to learn more about how well salt formations can serve as repository hosts. The results of these studies may prove of particular value to the United States in solving or easing the difficulties being experienced by the federal repository in New Mexico. As you will recall from Chapter Seven, the New Mexico facility is situated in a salt formation.

Still another example: Canada and the United States are cooperating in the construction of an underground research laboratory in a granite formation near Manitoba, Canada. When completed and in operation, the laboratory will undertake experiments that should help the two countries better understand and predict how well waste containers will perform in a granite repository.

The feasibility of subseabed disposal of nuclear wastes (see Chapter Five) is the subject of considerable international research. Many of these studies are being coordinated by the Seabed Working Group, which was formed in 1976. The group is made up of representatives from Canada, the Commission of European Communities, France, Great Britain, Japan, the Netherlands, Switzerland, the United States, and West Germany. Although the United States abandoned the idea of subseabed disposal some years ago, it maintains its membership in the group because it is interested in the scientific data expected to emerge from the group's research.

All knowledge garnered through the various international studies is to be made available to every nuclear nation. The problems and dangers involved in the safe disposal of nuclear wastes are worldwide and must be equally shared on a worldwide basis for the well-being of us all.

GLOSSARY

Alpha radiation: One of the three principal radiations emitted by radioactive substances. The radiations are made up of electrically charged particles that consist of two neutrons and two protons. Their eletrical charge is positive. They are unable to penetrate clothing or the outer layer of skin.

Atom: The basic building block of all matter. It is the smallest part of an element, and has all the chemical properties of that element. It consists of protons and neutrons in the nucleus, plus electrons.

Atomic half-life: The length of time it takes half the atoms in a radioactive substance to decay.

Atomic number: The number of protons in an atom.

Background radiation: Radiation from natural radioactive materials always present in the environment. Included are radiations from the sun, the ground, the atmosphere, building materials, and the bodies of humans and animals.

Beta radiation: One of the three principal radiations emitted by radioactive substances. They are composed of electrically charged particles. Their charge is negative. The particles have mass and charge equal to that of electrons. They have little ability to penetrate other materials.

Canister: The container in which high-level wastes are placed for permanent burial.

Cask: The container in which high-level wastes are transported to final burial.

Chain reaction: A self-sustaining series of nuclear fissions occurring in a reactor core. The neutrons that are released in one fission cause the next fission in the series to take place.

Commercial wastes: Radioactive wastes generated in the production of nuclear energy for commercial purposes. Commercial production can produce both high- and low-level wastes.

Curie: A measure of the rate at which radioactivity decays. It is equal to the radioactivity of one gram of radium or 37 billion disintegrations per second. The curie was named after Madame Marie Curie, who was the first scientist to study the radioactivity of uranium.

Defense wastes: Radioactive wastes generated in the production of nuclear energy for defense purposes. The wastes are generated in a variety of activities, including weapons research and development, the reprocessing of spent fuels, the operation of reactors on nuclear-powered ships and submarines, and the decommissioning of those vessels. The wastes are also known as government wastes.

Electrons: Electrically charged particles which revolve around the atomic nucleus. The electrical charge is negative.

Fission: The process of generating a nuclear reaction by splitting or breaking open atoms of heavy weight, such as those in uranium.

Fuel assemblies: The units into which fuel rods are bundled for insertion in a nuclear reactor.

Fuel rods: The stainless steel or zirconium tubes into which uranium pellets are placed for insertion into a nuclear reactor.

Fusion: The process of generating a nuclear reaction by joining the nuclei of certain atoms rather than splitting them as is done in fissioning.

Gamma radiation: One of the three principal radiations emitted by radioactive substances.

Mass number: The number of neutrons and protons in an atom. The mass number of uranium-238, for example, is 238, consisting of 146 neutrons and 92 protons.

Millirem: One-thousandth of a rem. See Rem.

Nucleus: The case of an atom, made up of protons and neutrons.

Neutrons: Uncharged particles found in the nucleus of every atom heavier than hydrogen.

Nuclide: A type of atom characterized by the makeup of its nucleus— namely, by the number of protons and neutrons and the energy content in the nucleus.

Plutonium: A radioactive element produced during the fissioning process. In its separated form, it can be made into either nuclear fuel or a nuclear explosive.

Protons: Electrically charged particles in the nucleus of an atom. Their electrical charge is positive.

Radiation: The process of emitting radiant energy in the form of waves or particles.

Radionuclides: Nuclides that are radioactive. See Nuclides.

Radioactivity: The spontaneous emission of alpha or beta and sometimes gamma radiation from the nucleus of an atom.

Reactor: The device in which atoms are fissioned. Also known in the past as an atomic furnace.

Reactor core: The heart of the nuclear reactor—the area in which fissioning takes place.

Rem: The unit used to measure the amount of damage to human tissue from a dose of radiation.

Repository: An installation for the permanent storage of high-level and/or low-level nuclear wastes. It is usually an underground facility. It can also be called a depository.

Reprocessing: The process of chemically removing uranium and plutonium from nuclear fuel rods so that the two elements can be reused.

Shielding: Material that successfully shields human beings and the environment from radiation. The materials best used for the shielding of high-level nuclear wastes are lead, concrete, steel, and water.

Spent fuel: Nuclear fuel that has been so saturated with radioactivity while in a reactor that it no longer performs efficiently in the chain reaction.

TNT: The acronym for trinotrotuluene, a type of high explosive.

Uranium: A slightly radioactive element employed in the production of nuclear energy. Its atomic number is 92.

SOURCE NOTES

Chapter 1
The Nuclear Age

1. The text and footnote material on the Hiroshima and Nagasaki bombings, the Alamogordo atomic test, and the hydrogen bomb are developed from C. E. Cobb, Jr., "Living With Radiation," *National Geographic* (April 1989): 407, and *The 1989 Information Please Almanac* (Boston: Houghton Mifflin, 1989), 375.

2. The material on the nature of nuclear energy and its production by the fission and fusion methods is developed from: information supplied to the authors by D. Bhadra, physicist, General Atomic Company, San Diego, California; N. Hawkes, *Nuclear Safety* (New York: Gloucester Press, 1987), 8, 12; R. McKown, *The Fabulous Isotopes* (New York: Holiday House, 1962), 179; G. J. O'Neill, "Nuclear Power: Today . . . Tomorrow," *The Lion* (December 1988/ January 1989): 8; *The 1989 Information Please Almanac,* 375–76.

3. The material on the nations that use nuclear energy for the production of electrical power is developed from: Cobb, 421; L. Martz, "The Nuclear Bargain," *Newsweek* (May 12, 1986): 44; Hawkes, 7; O'Neill, 43; *World Almanac and Book of Facts 1986* (New York: Newspaper Enterprise Association, 1986), 125.

4. The material on nuclear energy as a valuable power source and medical tool is developed from: L. R. Brown, Project Director, *State of the World, 1989: A Worldwatch Institute Report on Progress*

Toward a Sustainable Society (New York: W. W. Norton, 1989), 9; Cobb, 421; Hawkes, 7; "New Pacemaker Patient Says He Feels Fine," *San Francisco Chronicle* (from United Press), November 11, 1988.

5. The text and footnote material on radioactivity and its dangers are developed from: Cobb, 406, 418–19; Hawkes, 11; *Answers to Your Questions on High-Level Nuclear Waste* (Washington, D.C.: Office of Civilian Radioactive Waste Management [OCRWM], U.S. Department of Energy, 1987), 4, 7; "Radiation and High-Level Radioactive Waste, *OCRWM Backgrounder* (May 1988): 2; San Diego Section, American Nuclear Society, *Questions and Answers: Nuclear Power and the Environment* (San Diego, California: Gulf General Atomic Company, 1972), 10–12.

6. The material on the Chernobyl reactor accident is developed from: S. Begley, "The 20th-Century Plague," *Newsweek* (May 12, 1986); Brown, 5, 69; O'Neill, 8; D. Perlman, "New Chernobyl Predictions —Lower Risk of Death, Disease," *San Francisco Chronicle*, December 17, 1988; "Crisis at Soviet Nuclear Plant Spreads Radiation, Fear: Moscow Admits Two Deaths, Says Problem Under Control," *Facts on File,* May 2, 1986, 305; "Cancer Rate Soaring in Area Near Chernobyl," *San Francisco Chronicle* (from Associated Press), February 16, 1989.

7. The material on U.S. reactor accidents is developed from: Hawkes, 21; O'Neill, 7; *Facts,* May 2, 1986, 307; *Completing the Task* (Washington, D.C.: U.S. Council for Energy Awareness, 1988), 1; "Cleansing the Atom," *Life* (March 1989): 20.

Chapter 2
It's Called Radwaste

1. The material on the origin of nuclear wastes is developed from: *Answers to Your Questions on High-Level Nuclear Waste* (Washington, D.C.: Office of Civilian Radioactive Waste Management [OCRWM], U.S. Department of Energy, 1987), 1.

2. The material on the ways in which the wastes have been affected by radioactivity is developed from: information supplied to the authors by D. Bhadra, physicist, General Atomic Company, San Diego, California; N. Hawkes, *Nuclear Safety* (New York: Gloucester Press, 1987), 8; The League of Women Voters Education Fund (LWVEF), *The Nuclear Waste Primer: A Handbook for Citizens* (New York: Nick Lyons Books, 1985), 9; *Managing the Nation's Nuclear Waste,* (Washington, D.C.: OCRWM, U. S. Department of Energy, undated), 1.

3. The text and footnote material on the four types of nuclear waste and their radiation emissions is developed from: Bhadra; C. E. Cobb, Jr., "Living With Radiation," *National Geographic* (April 1989): 412–13, 415; San Diego Section, American Nuclear Society, *Questions and Answers: Nuclear Power and the Environment* (San Diego, California: Gulf General Atomic Company, 1972), 7–8; LWVEF, 8–9, 37; OCRWM, *Answers,* 1–5; OCRWM, *Managing,* 1.

4. The material on the accumulation of the waste materials over the years is developed from: Bhadra; Cobb, 428; LWVEF, 1–2; OCRWM, *Answers,* 2, 5; OCRWM, *Managing,* 2.

Chapter 3
The Blind Years

1. The material on the early lack of understanding concerning the dangers of nuclear waste is developed from: L. Martz, "The Nuclear Bargain," *Newsweek* (May 12, 1988): 41–42; K. Schneider, "U.S. Studies Health Problems Near Weapon Plant," *New York Times,* October 17, 1988; F. C. Shapiro, *Radwaste* (New York: Random House, 1981), 18–19; F. C. Shapiro, "A Reporter at Large: Yucca Mountain," *New Yorker* (May 23, 1988): 67.

2. The material on the Parkersburg incident is developed from: A. K. Naj, "Can $100 Billion Have 'No Material Effect' on Balance Sheets?" *Wall Street Journal,* May 11, 1988.

3. The material on the waste disposal problems at the Hanford plant is developed from: J. Cramer, "They Lied to Us," *Time* (October 31, 1988): 63–64; "Hanford Firm: N-Waste Leaks Unavoidable," *Seattle Times/Seattle Post Intelligencer* (from Associated Press), January 29, 1988; Schneider.

4. The material on the waste disposal problems at the Fernald plant is developed from: Cramer, 61–62; K. B. Noble, "Bitter Neighborhood Adjoins U.S. Uranium Plant in Ohio," *New York Times,* October 19, 1988; "A Deadly Secret," a segment of the ABC news program, "20/20," March 26, 1987, transcript pages 10–13; "U.S. Ignored A-Plant's Tons of Toxic Emissions," *San Francisco Chronicle* (from *New York Times),* October 15, 1988; "Ohio Wants Shoddy Uranium Plant Shut," *San Francisco Chronicle* (from Associated Press), October 19, 1988.

5. The material on present waste storage systems is developed from: information supplied to the authors by D. Bhadra, physicist, General Atomic Company, San Diego, California; The League of Women Voters Education Fund, *The Nuclear Waste Primer: A Handbook for Citizens* (New York: Nick Lyons Books, 1985), 33–

34; *Answers to Your Questions on High-Level Nuclear Waste* (Washington, D.C.: Office of Civilian Radioactive Waste Management, U.S. Department of Energy, 1987), 5.

Chapter 4
Storing the Low-Level Wastes

1. The material on the Low-Level Radioactive Waste Policy Act is developed from: The League of Women Voters Education Fund (LWVEF), *The Nuclear Waste Primer: A Handbook for Citizens* (New York: Nick Lyons Books, 1985), 57; L. Martz, "The Nuclear Bargain," *Newsweek* (May 12, 1986): 40.
2. The material on the disposal of liquid low-level wastes by ground percolation, deep well injection, and grout injection is developed from: information supplied to the authors by D. Bhadra, physicist, General Atomic Company, San Diego, California; "Studies of Alternative Methods of Radioactive Waste Disposal," *OCRWM* (Office of Civilian Radioactive Waste Management) *Backgrounder* (April 1987): 3.
3. The material on the disposal of solid low-level wastes by sea dumping is developed from: Bhadra; F. C. Shapiro, *Radwaste* (New York: Random House, 1981), 122–23; "The Deep," a segment of the ABC news program, "20/20," February 24, 1987, transcript pages 12–13.
4. The material on the sea dumping of medical wastes is developed from: "New Rules Limit Medical Waste Dumping, *San Francisco Chronicle*, August 11, 1988; R. Spafford, "Toxic Territory," *San Francisco Chronicle*, June 25, 1989.
5. The material on the disposal of solid low-level wastes by shallow land burial is developed from: Bhadra; Shapiro, 3–6.
6. The material on the disposal of solid low-level wastes in mined cavities is developed from: Bhadra.
7. The material on the state compacts is developed from: LWVEF, 58.

Chapter 5
Corrosion, Leaks, and Ideas

1. The text and footnote material on the storage of high-level wastes at Hanford, Savannah River, and Idaho Falls government plants from the 1940s to the early 1970s is developed from: The League of Women Voters Education Fund (LWVEF), *The Nuclear Waste Primer: A Handbook for Citizens* (New York: Nick Lyons Books, 1985), 27–29.

2. The material on research into leakage and sludge removal problems at Hanford and Savannah, plus the decontamination work being done at West Valley is developed from: LWVEF, 28–29.

3. The material on the methods of high-level waste disposal that have been considered through the years by the DOE is developed from: information supplied to the authors by D. Bhadra, physicist, General Atomic Company, San Diego, California; "Studies of Alternative Methods of Radioactive Waste Disposal," *OCRWM* (Office of Civilian Radioactive Waste Management) *Backgrounder* (April 1987): 1–4; F. C. Shapiro, "A Reporter at Large: Yucca Mountain," *New Yorker* (May 23, 1988): 64; LWVEF, 64–66.

Chapter 6
An Act and a Search

1. The material on the specific points in the Nuclear Waste Policy Act is developed from: *Draft 1988 Mission Plan Amendment* (Washington, D.C.: Office of Civilian Radioactive Waste Management [OCRWM], U.S. Department of Energy, 1988), 1; The League of Women Voters Education Fund, *The Nuclear Waste Primer: A Handbook for Citizens* (New York: Nick Lyons Books, 1985), 55–56; "NRC and DOE Sign Memorandum of Understanding for Cost Recovery," *OCRWM Bulletin,* August 1988, 1–2; *Answers to Your Questions on High-Level Nuclear Waste* (Washington, D.C.: OCRWM, U.S. Department of Energy, 1987), 6; *Managing the Nation's Nuclear Waste* (Washington, D.C.: OSRWM, U.S. Department of Energy, undated), 3, 8.

2. The material on the rights granted to the states and Indian tribes under the terms of the Nuclear Waste Policy Act is developed from: OCRWM, *Answers,* 46–47.

3. The material on the assignments given to various federal agencies under the terms of the Nuclear Waste Policy Act is developed from: OCRWM, *Answers,* 6–7.

4. The material describing the planned repository is developed from: D. Grossman and S. Shulman, "A Nuclear Dump: The Experiment Begins," *Discover* (March 1989): 50; R. Monastersky, "The 10,000-Year Test," *Science News* (February 27, 1988): 141; OCRWM, *Answers,* 15–17; OCRWM, *Managing,* 4.

5. The material on the difficulties involved in the search for the repository site is developed from: F. C. Shapiro, "A Reporter at Large: Yucca Mountain," *New Yorker* (May 23, 1988): 62; OCRWM, *Answers,* 14; LWVEF, 64.

6. The material on the provisions in the Nuclear Waste Policy Amendments Act is developed from: *Title V—Energy and Environment Programs: Subtitle A—Nuclear Waste Amendments,* unabridged excerpts from the Amendments Act (Washington, D.C.: OCRWM, U.S. Department of Energy, undated), 237–249, 255–256; OCRWM, *Answers,* 6; OCRWM, *Managing,* 3.

7. The material on Deaf Smith County, Hanford, and Yucca Mountain is developed from: Grossman and Shulman, 51; Monastersky, 139; Shapiro, 63.

Chapter 7
The Place Called Yucca Mountain

1. The description of Yucca Mountain and its surroundings is developed from: D. Grossman and S. Shulman, "A Nuclear Dump: The Experiment Begins," *Discover* (March 1989): 51; M. L. Wald, "Unsettling Questions as U.S. Tries to Build A-Waste Repository," *San Francisco Chronicle* (from *New York Times),* January 17, 1989; F. C. Shapiro, "A Reporter at Large: Yucca Mountain," *New Yorker* (May 23, 1988): 61–62.

2. The description of the repository is developed from: Grossman and Shulman, 49–51; R. Monastersky, "The 10,000-Year Test," *Science News* (February 27, 1988): 141; *Draft 1988 Mission Plan Amendment* (Washington, D.C.: Office of Civilian Radioactive Waste Management [OCRWM], U.S. Department of Energy, 1988), 36–38.

3. The material on the schedule for the planning and construction of the repository is developed from: OCRWM, *Draft 1988 Mission Plan,* 24, 51; "Nevada Refuses U.S. Requests for Nuclear Waste Permits," *San Francisco Chronicle* (from Reuters), December 27, 1989.

4. The material on the Nevada opposition to and support of the proposed repository is developed from: K. Davidson, "Nevadans Fuming over Atomic Dump," *San Francisco Examiner/Chronicle,* August 14, 1988; Grossman and Shulman, 51; Shapiro, 63, 64, 66; "Nevada Declaring Nuclear Waste Dump Against the Law," *San Francisco Chronicle* (from *Los Angeles Times),* June 30, 1989; "Nevada Sues U.S. to Block Nuclear Dump," *San Francisco Chronicle* (from Reuters), December 28, 1989.

5. The material and footnotes on the host-rock, water, volcanic, and earthquake characterization studies at Yucca Mountain is developed from: Grossman and Shulman, 49, 51, 54–56; Monastersky, 139–141; Shapiro, 65–66; OCRWM, *Draft 1988 Mission Plan,* 25–26.

Chapter 8
The Road to Burial

1. The material on how the transportation system and the MRS unit will work together is developed from: *Draft 1988 Mission Plan Amendment* (Washington, D.C.: Office of Civilian Radioactive Waste Management [OCRWM], U.S. Department of Energy, 1986), 39; *Transporting Spent Nuclear Fuel: An Overview* (Washington, D.C.: OCRWM, U.S. Department of Energy, 1986), 9–10; *Managing the Nation's Nuclear Waste* (Washington, D.C.: OCRWM, U.S. Department of Energy, undated), 8.

2. The material on why the MRS unit is necessary in the transportation plan is developed from: OCRWM, *Draft 1988 Mission Plan,* 39–40; OCRWM *Transporting,* 7.

3. The material on the three major agencies responsible for transportation of the wastes is developed from: *Answers to Your Questions on Nuclear High-Level Nuclear Waste* (Washington, D.C.: OCRWM, U.S. Department of Energy, 1987), 20; *Transportation Institutional Plan: Executive Summary* (Washington, D.C.: OCRWM, U.S. Department of Energy, 1987), 2–4; OCRWM, *Transporting,* 7.

4. The material on construction and testing of shipping casks is developed from: "Health and Safety Protection in the Management of the Nation's High-Level Radioactive Wastes, *OCRWM Backgrounder* (May 1988): 2–3; OCRWM, *Answers,* 20–21, 22, 23; OCRWM, *Draft 1988 Mission Plan,* 41–42; OCRWM, *Transportation,* 1; OCRWM, *Transporting,* 13–15.

5. The material on the methods of transportation is developed from: OCRWM, *Answers,* 4; OCRWM, *Transporting,* 7.

6. The material on a typical truck shipment from a power plant to the MRS unit is developed from: F. C. Shapiro, *Radwaste* (New York: Random House, 1981), 263; OCRWM, *Answers,* 23–24; OCRWM, *Transporting,* 9–10.

7. The material on the MRS unit, its facilities, and its work is developed from: The League of Women Voters Education Fund, *The Nuclear Waste Primer: A Handbook for Citizens* (New York: Nick Lyons Books, 1985), 55–56; OCRWM, *Answers,* 26–28; OCRWM, *Draft 1988 Mission Plan,* 39–41, 51, 52.

8. The material on the final burial of the wastes at the repository is developed from: information supplied to the authors by Battelle, Pacific Northwest Laboratories, Richland, Washington; "The Multiple Barrier System of Geologic Disposal of Spent Nuclear Fuel and High-Level Radioactive Waste," *OCRWM Backgrounder,* (May 1988): 3.

9. The material on plans for steps to be taken when the repository is filled to capacity is developed from: OCRWM, *Answers,* 35–36.

Chapter 9
The World Story

1. The material on the nuclear nations and their plans for the disposal of high-level wastes is developed from: N. Hawkes, *Nuclear Safety* (New York: Gloucester Press, 1987), 31; League of Women Voters Education Fund (LWVEF), *The Nuclear Waste Primer: A Handbook for Citizens* (New York: Nick Lyons Books, 1985), 73; L. Martz, "The Nuclear Bargain," *Newsweek* (May 12, 1986): 44; G. J. O'Neill, "Nuclear Power: Today . . . Tomorrow," *The Lion* (December 1988/January 1989): 43; *International Cooperation Program* (Washington, D.C.: Office of Civilian Radioactive Waste Management [OCRWM], U.S. Department of Energy, 1986), 1–10.
2. The material on foreign reprocessing and the disposal of low-level wastes is developed from: LWVEF, 68; OCRWM, 9.
3. The material on international tensions and problems arising out of nuclear energy and waste is developed from: L. R. Brown, Project Director, *State of the World, 1989: A Worldwatch Institute Report on Progress Toward a Sustainable Society* (New York: W. W. Norton, 1989), 144; N. Sheppard, Jr., "Toxic Waste a Growing U.S. Export," *San Francisco Examiner* (from *Chicago Tribune),* July 17, 1988.
4. The material on the international cooperative researches into nuclear waste is developed from: LWVEF, 71–72; OCRWM, 10–11.

BIBLIOGRAPHY

Books

Ardley, Neil. *Atoms and Energy* (Updated Edition). New York: Warwick Press, 1982.

Brown, Lester R. *State of the World, 1989: A Worldwatch Institute Report on Progress Toward a Sustainable Society.* New York: W. W. Norton, 1989.

Hawkes, Nigel. *Nuclear Safety.* New York: Gloucester Press, 1987.

League of Women Voters Education Fund, The. *The Nuclear Waste Primer: A Handbook for Citizens.* New York: Nick Lyons Books, 1985.

McKown, Robin. *The Fabulous Isotopes.* New York: Holiday House, 1962.

Moche, Dinah. *Radiation.* New York: Franklin Watts, 1979.

Newhouse, John. *War and Peace in the Nuclear Age.* New York: Alfred A. Knopf, 1989.

Poch, David I. *Radiation Alert.* New York: Doubleday, 1985.

Robinson, Marilynne. *Mother Country.* New York: Farrar, Straus & Giroux, 1989.

Shapiro, Fred C. *Radwaste.* New York: Random House, 1981.

Magazine Articles

Begley, Sharon. "The 20th Century Plague," *Newsweek,* May 12, 1986.

Church, George J. "Playing Atomic NIMBY," *Time,* December 26, 1988.

Cobb, Charles E., Jr. "Living With Radiation," *National Geographic*, April 1989.

Cook, William J. "Nuclear Power, Act II," *U.S. News and World Report*," May 29, 1989.

Cramer, Jerome; Leavitt, Russell, B.; and Nash, J. Madeleine. "They Lied to Us," *Time*, October 31, 1988.

"Crisis at Soviet Nuclear Plant Spreads Radiation, Fear: Moscow Admits Two Deaths, Says Problem Under Control," *Facts on File*, May 2, 1986.

Grossman, Dan and Shulman, Seth. "A Nuclear Dump: The Experiment Begins," *Discover*, March 1989.

Martz, Larry. "The Nuclear Bargain," *Newsweek*, May 12, 1986.

Monastersky, Richard. "The 10,000-Year Test," *Science News*, February 27, 1988.

O'Neill, George J. "Nuclear Power: Today . . . Tomorrow," *The Lion*, December 1988–January 1989.

Schiavo, Frank R. "A Dose Is a Dose Is a Dose," *Sierra*, September/October 1986.

Shapiro, Fred C. "A Reporter at Large: Yucca Mountain," *New Yorker*, May 23, 1988.

Government Publications

The publications listed here were produced by the Office of Civilian Radioactive Waste Management, U.S. Department of Energy, Washington, D.C.

Answers to Your Questions on High-Level Nuclear Waste, 1987.

Draft 1988 Mission Plan Amendment, 1988.

International Cooperation Program, 1986.

Managing the Nation's Nuclear Waste, undated

OCRWM Transportation Program Reference, 1988.

Title V—Energy and Environment Programs: Subtitle A—Nuclear Waste Amendments, 1987.

Transportation Institutional Plan: Executive Summary, 1987.

Transporting Spent Nuclear Fuel: An Overview, 1986.

"Studies of Alternative Methods of Radioactive Waste Disposal," *OCRWM Backgrounder*, April 1987.

"Radiation and High-Level Radioactive Waste," *OCRWM Backgrounder*, May 1988.

"Health and Safety Protection in the Management of the Nation's High-Level Radioactive Waste," *OCRWM Backgrounder*, May 1988.

"The Multiple Barrier System of Geologic Disposal of Spent Nuclear Fuel and High-Level Radioactive Waste," *OCRWM Backgrounder,* May 1988.
"NRC and DOE Sign Memorandum of Understanding for Cost Recovery," *OCRWM Bulletin,* August 1988.

Newspaper Articles

"Cancer Rates Soaring in Area Near Chernobyl," *San Francisco Chronicle* (from Associated Press), February 16, 1989.
Davidson, Keay. "Nevadans Fuming over Atomic Dump," *San Francisco Examiner/Chronicle,* August 14, 1988.
"Hanford Firm: N-Waste Leaks Unavoidable," *Seattle Times/Seattle Post Intelligencer* (from Associated Press), January 29, 1988.
Luoma, Jon R. "U.S. Turning to New Technologies to Clean Up Arms Plants," *New York Times,* January 3, 1989.
Naj, Amal Kumar. "Can $100 Billion Have 'No Material Effect' on Balance Sheets?" *Wall Street Journal,* May 11, 1988.
"Nevada Declaring Nuclear Waste Dump Against the Law," *San Francisco Chronicle* (from *Los Angeles Times),* June 30, 1989.
"Nevada Refuses U.S. Requests for Nuclear Waste Permits," *San Francisco Chronicle* (from Reuters), December 27, 1989.
"Nevada Sues U.S. to Block Nuclear Dump," *San Francisco Chronicle* (from Reuters), December 28, 1989.
"New Pacemaker Patient Says He Feels Fine," *San Francisco Chronicle* (From United Press International), November 11, 1988.
"New Rules Limit Medical Waste Dumping," *San Francisco Chronicle,* August 11, 1988.
Noble, Kenneth B. "Bitter Neighborhood Adjoins U.S. Uranium Plant in Ohio," *New York Times,* October 19, 1988.
"Nuclear Dump's Opening Delayed," *San Francisco Chronicle,* September 14, 1988.
"Nuclear Waste Dump Site May Be Volcano-Prone," *San Francisco Chronicle* (from Associated Press), July 19, 1989.
"Ohio Wants Shoddy Uranium Plant Shut," *San Francisco Chronicle* (from Associated Press), October 19, 1988.
"Opening of N-Waste Dump in New Mexico Delayed," *Herald* (Everett, Washington), May 18, 1989.
Perlman, David. "New Chernobyl Predictions—Lower Risk of Death, Disease," *San Francisco Chronicle,* December 17, 1988.
Schneider, Keith. "Pressure Grows for Better Weapon-Plant Safety," *New York Times,* October 27, 1988.

Sheppards, Nathaniel, Jr. "Toxic Waste a Growing U.S. Export," *San Francisco Examiner* (from *Chicago Tribune)*, July 17, 1988.

Spafford, Roz. "Toxic Territory," *San Francisco Chronicle*, June 25, 1989.

"U.S. Ignored A-Plant's Tons of Toxic Emissions," *San Francisco Chronicle* (from *New York Times)*, October 15, 1988.

Wald, Matthew L. "Unsettling Questions as U.S. Tries to Build A-Waste Repository," *San Francisco Chronicle* (from *New York Times)*, January 17, 1989.

Booklets

San Diego Section, American Nuclear Society. *Questions and Answers: Nuclear Power and the Environment.* San Diego: Gulf General Atomic Company, 1972.

The Electric Companies' Nuclear Transportation Group in Cooperation with the U.S. Council for Energy Awareness. *Questions and Answers: Transporting Low-Level Radioactive Waste.* Washington, D.C., undated.

U.S. Council for Energy Awareness. *Completing the Task: Decommissioning Nuclear Power Plants.* Washington, D.C., 1988.

Television Transcripts

ABC News, "The Deep," a segment of the program "20/20," February 24, 1983.

ABC News, "A Deadly Secret," a segment of the program "20/20," March 26, 1987.

INDEX

DATE DUE

DEMCO 38-297